The Beautiful Women Coloring Book

By Mel Borges

Images Inspired by BEAUTIFUL WOMEN:

1. Aaliyah
2. Angelina Jolie
3. Ariana Grande
4. Audrey Hepburn
5. Bella Hadid
6. Beyoncé
7. Brigitte Bardot
8. Catherine Zeta-Jones
9. Christie Brinkley
10. Cindy Crawford
11. Coco Austin
12. Demi Lovato
13. Diana Ross
14. Dorothy Dandridge
15. Eva Marcille
16. Farrah Fawcett
17. Gal Gadot
18. Halle Berry
19. Jada Pinkett Smith
20. Janet Jackson
21. Jennifer Lopez
22. Jessica Alba
23. Kim Kardashian
24. Lisa Raye McCoy
25. Marilyn Monroe
26. Mila Kunis
27. Naomi Campbell
28. Pam Grier
29. Raquel Welch
30. Rhianna
31. Sade Adu
32. Salma Hayek
33. Scarlett Johansson
34. Shakira
35. Sofia Vergara
36. Sophia Loren
37. Stacy Dash
38. Taylor Swift
39. Tyra Banks
40. Vanessa Williams

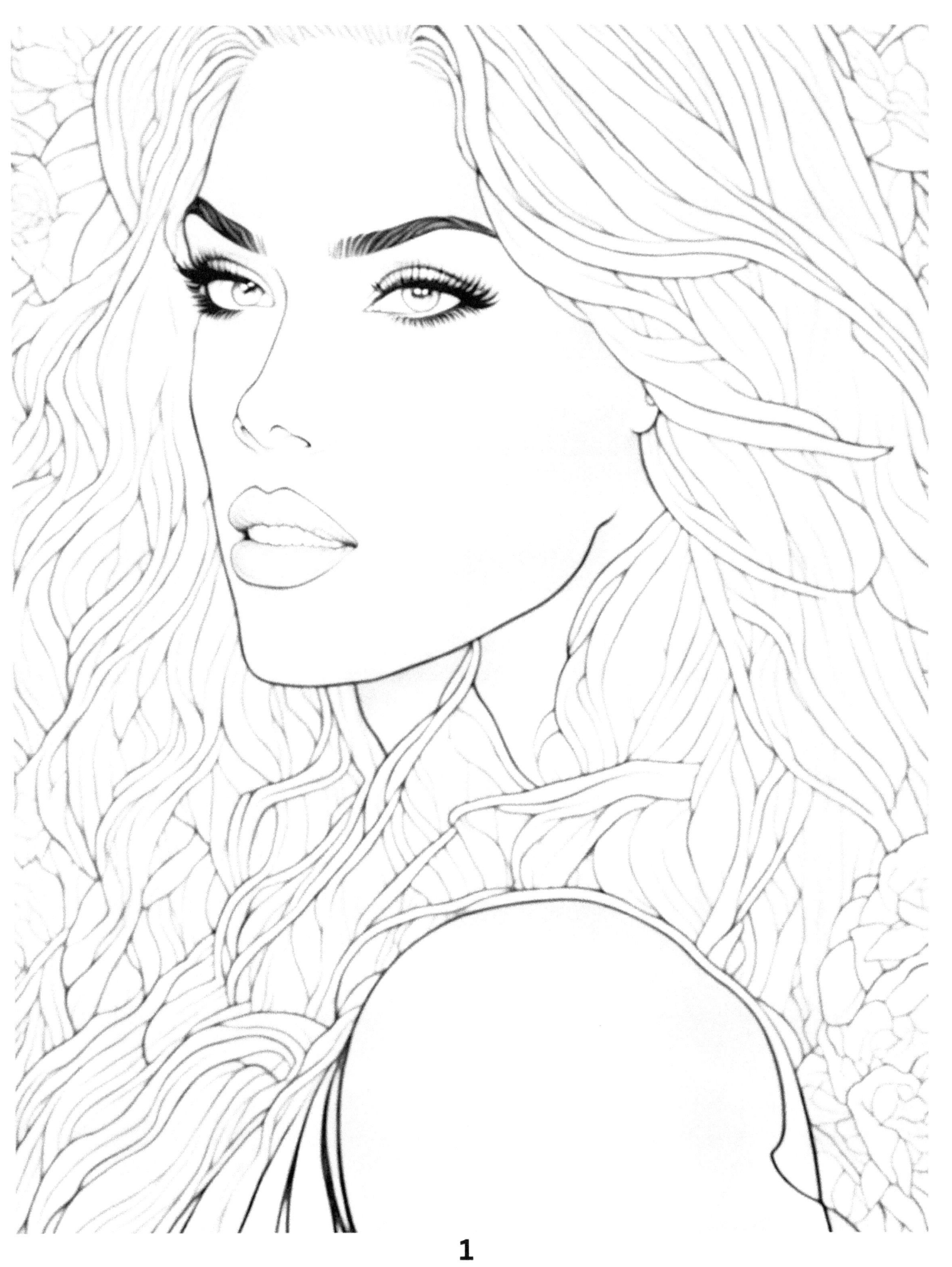

1

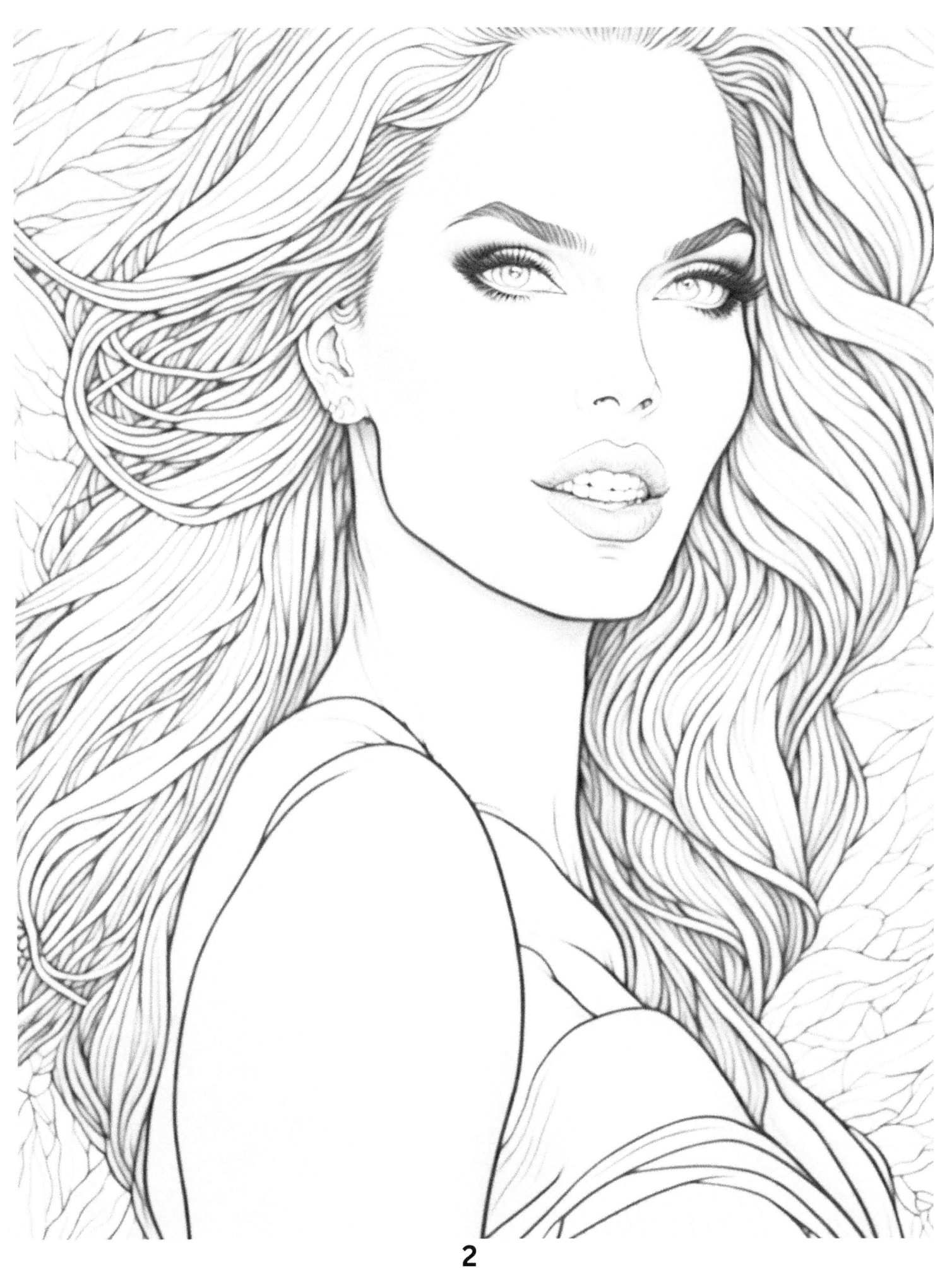

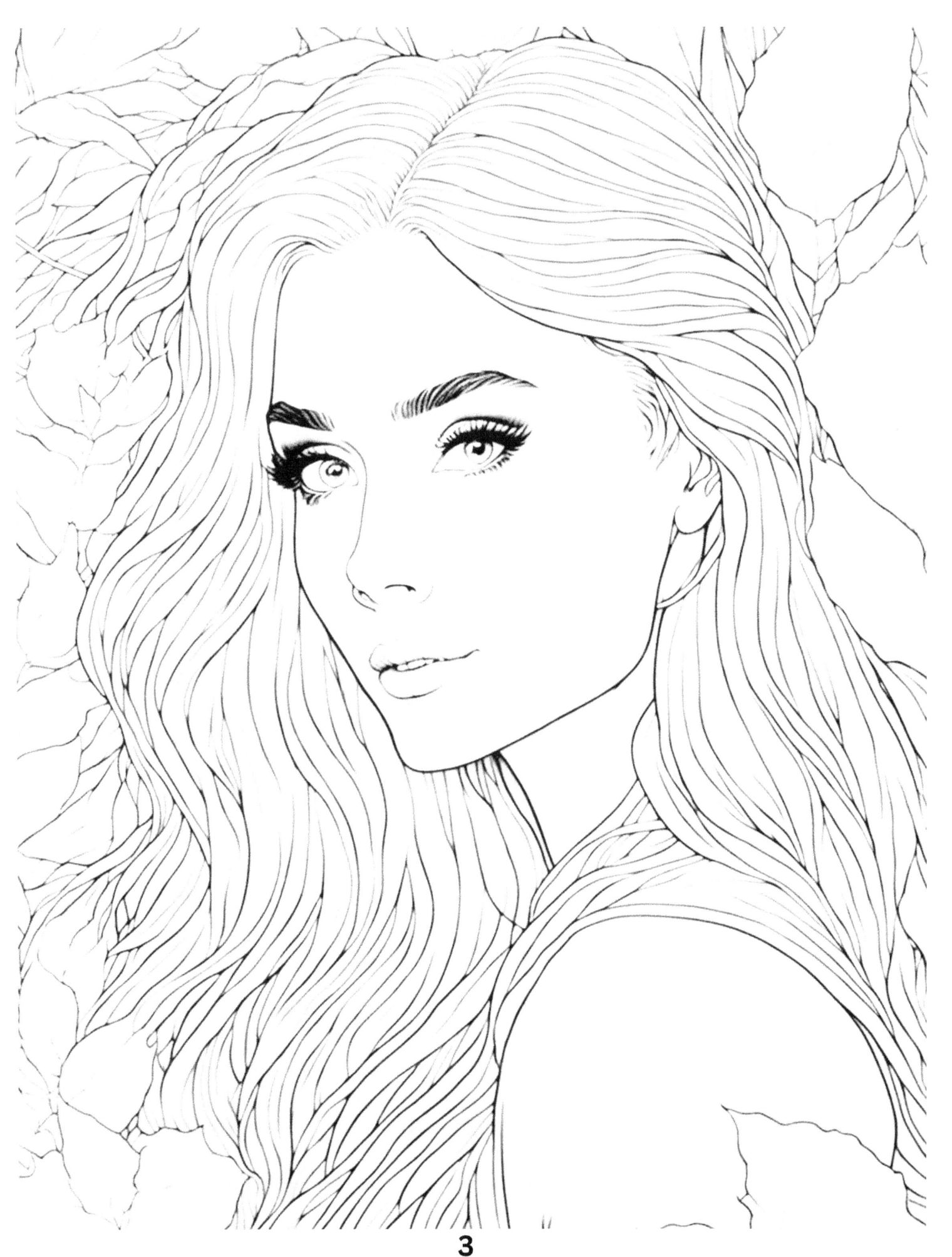

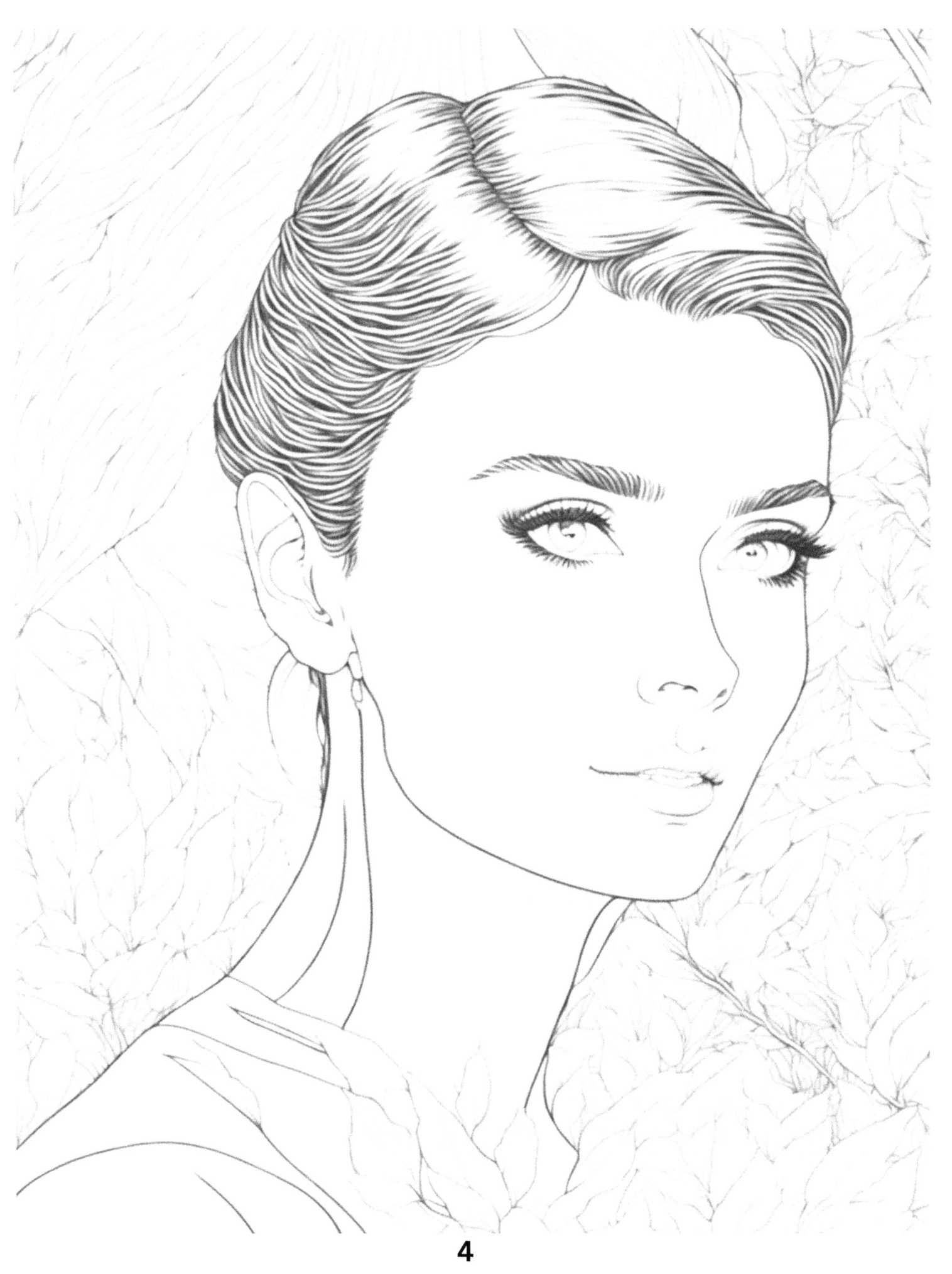

4

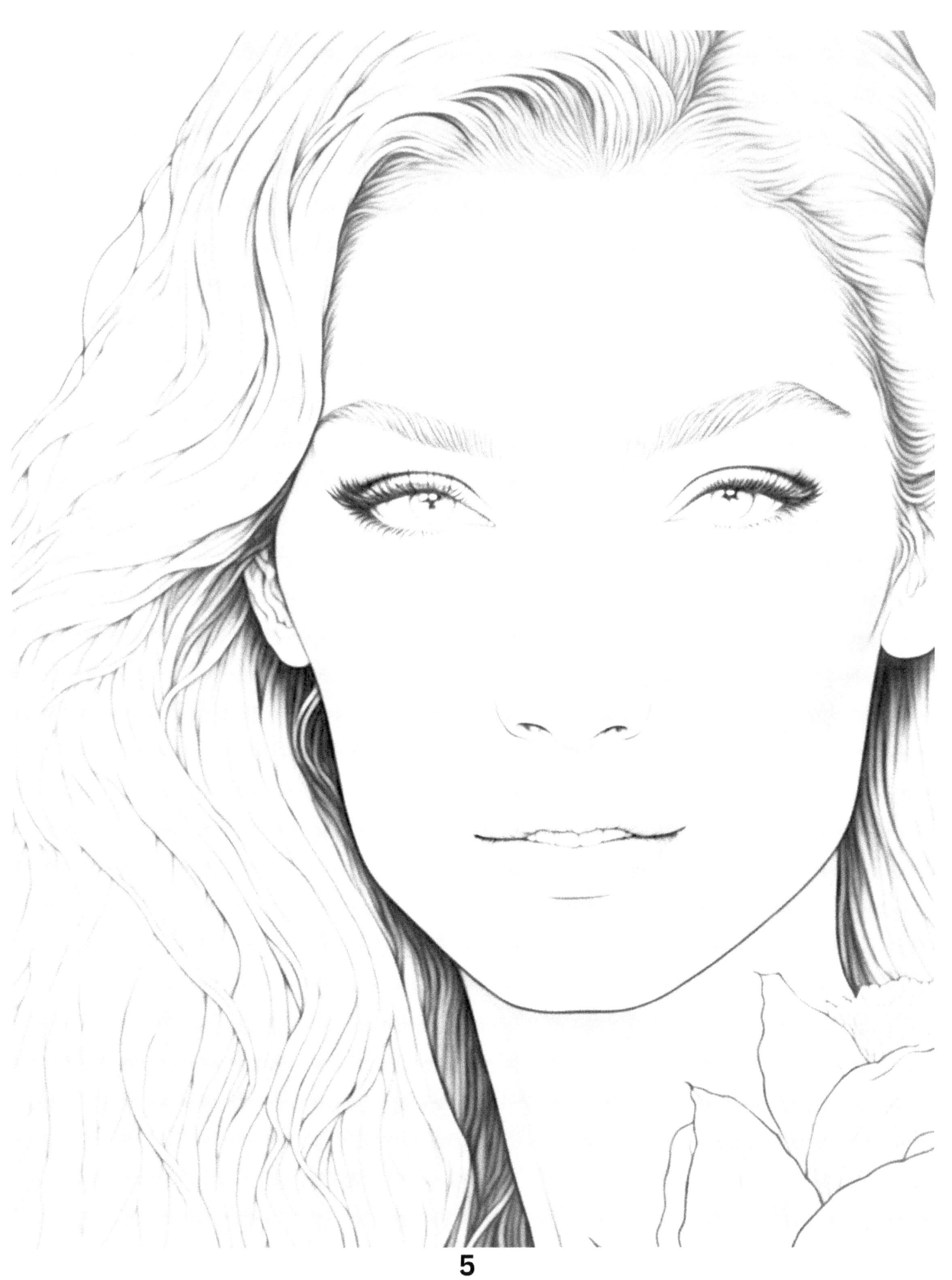

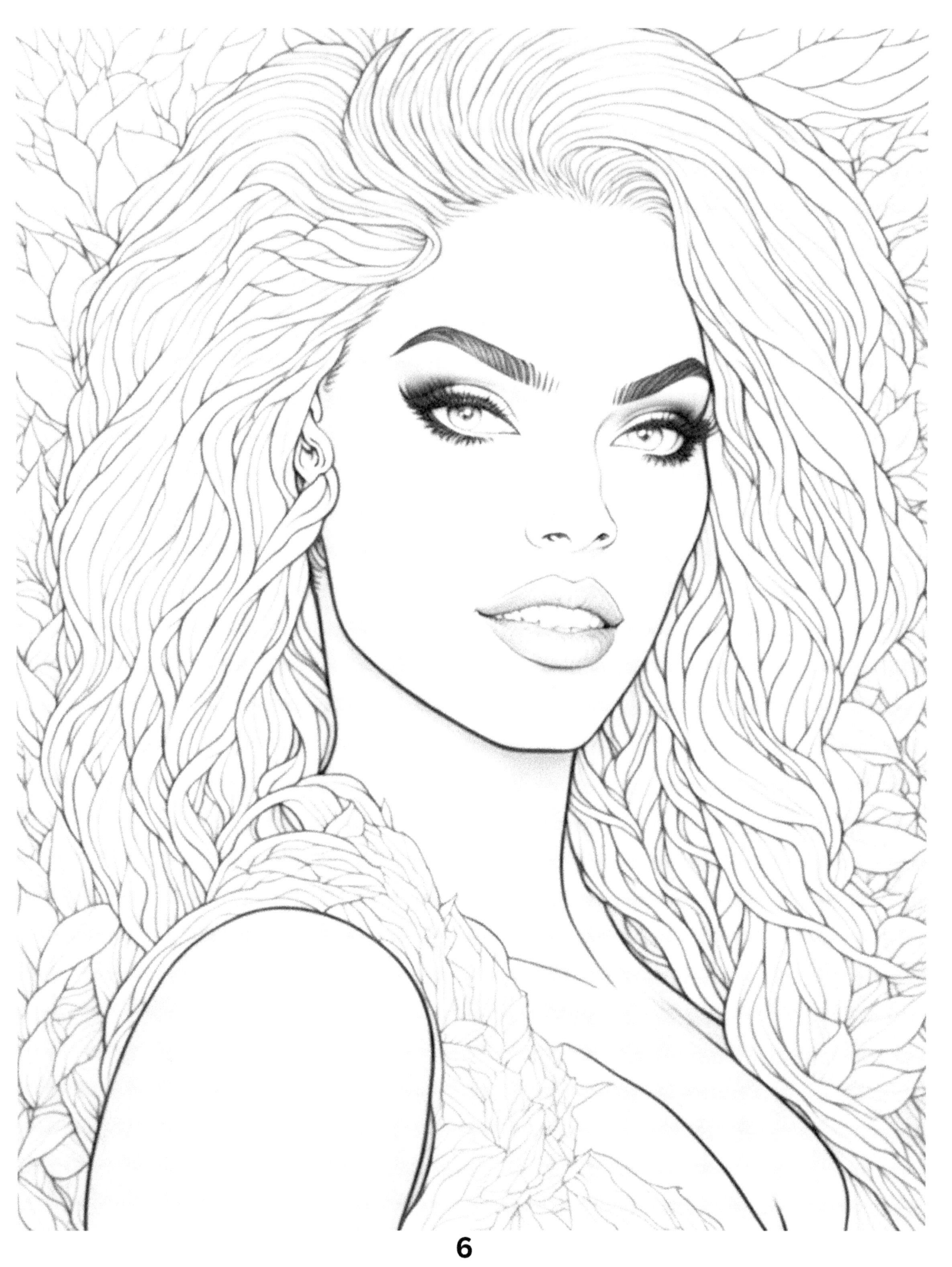

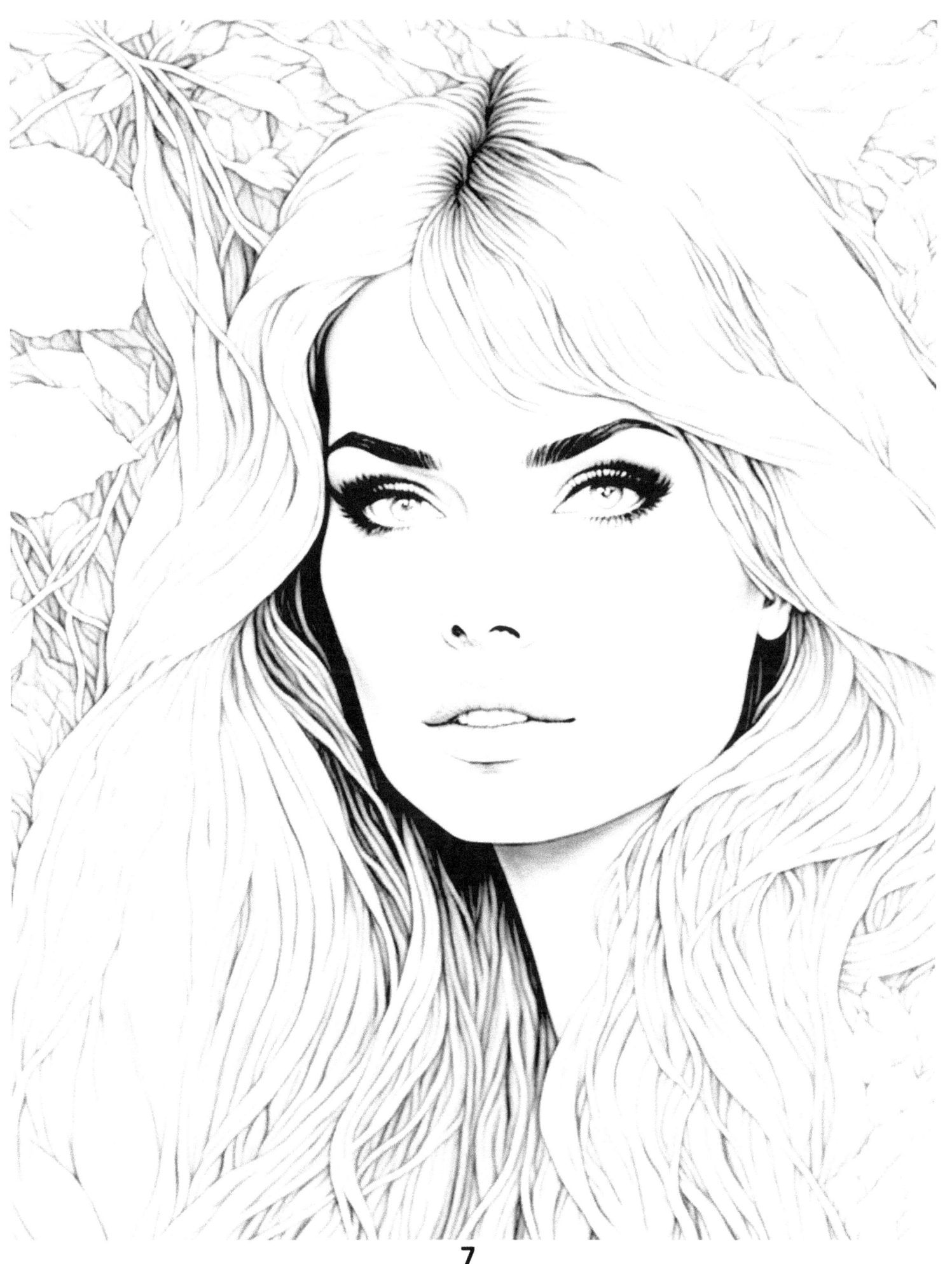

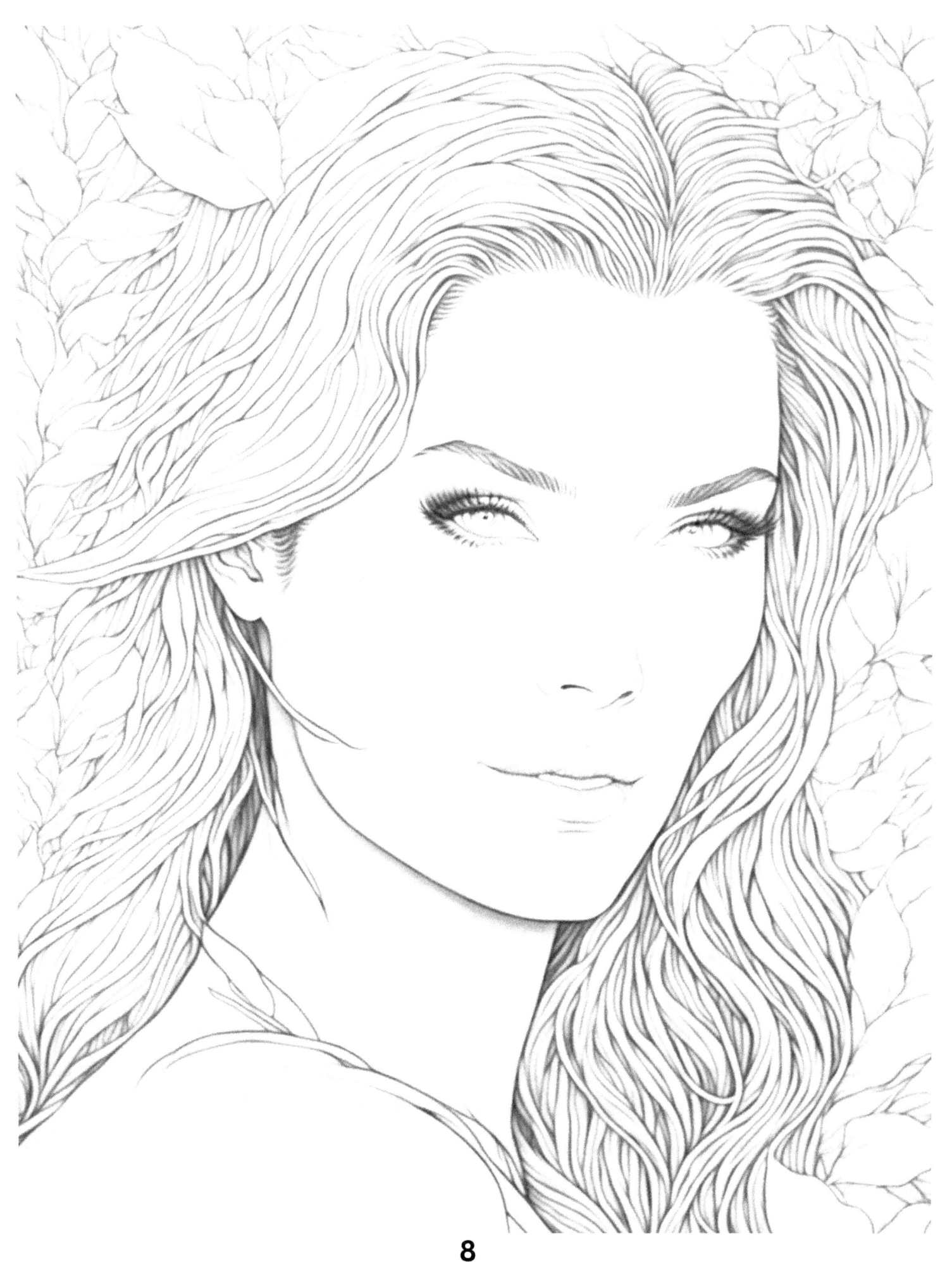

8

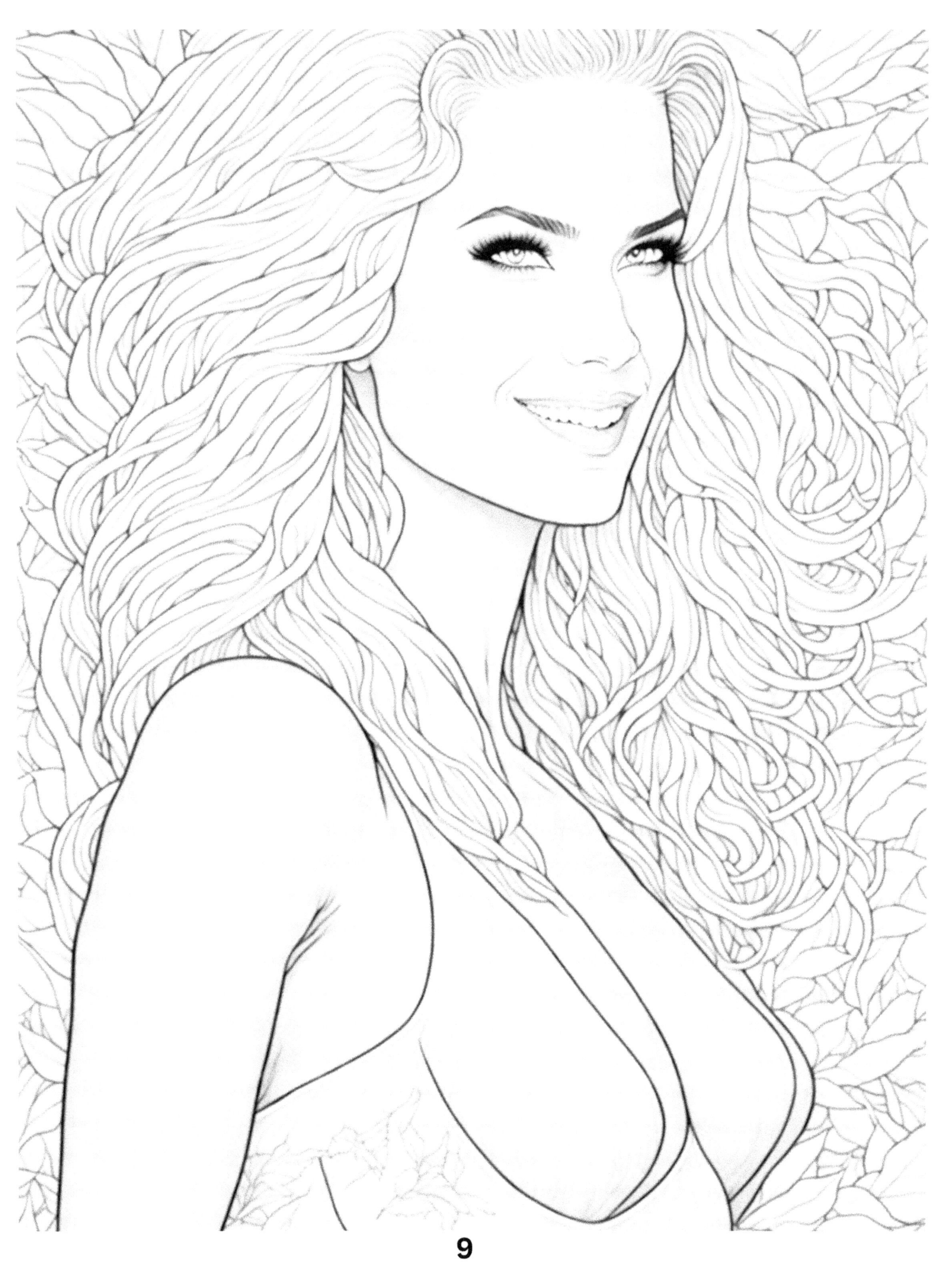

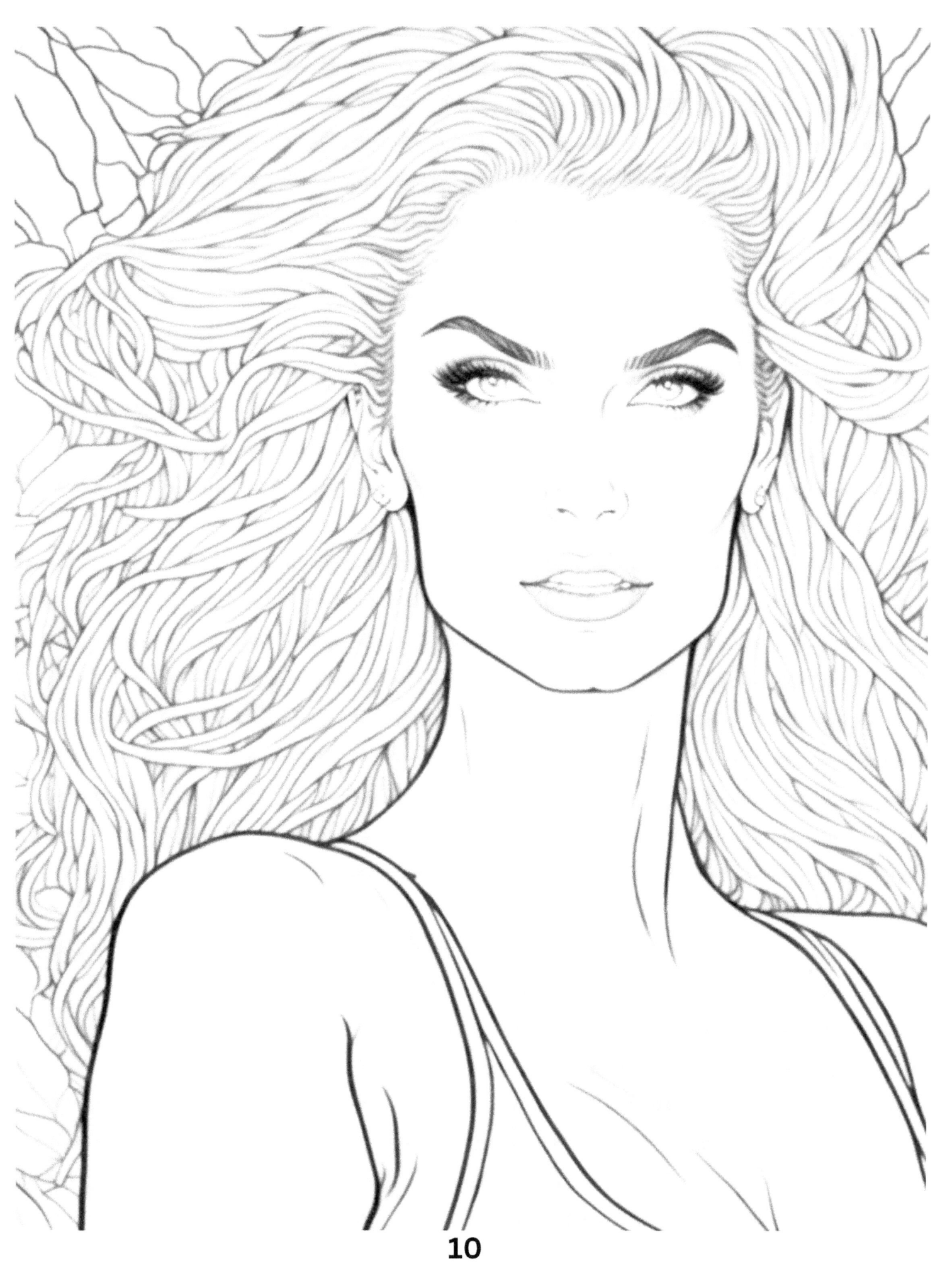

10

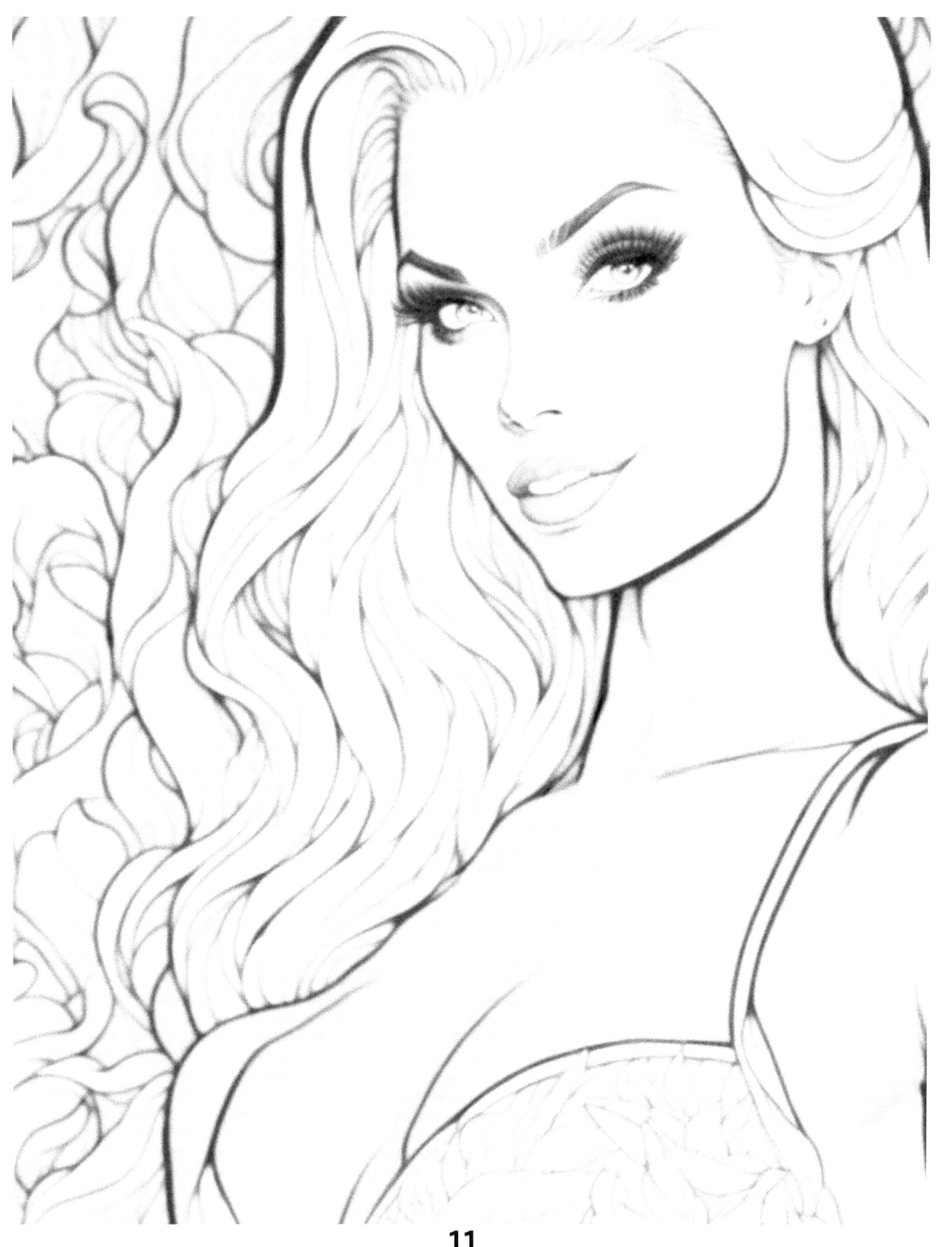

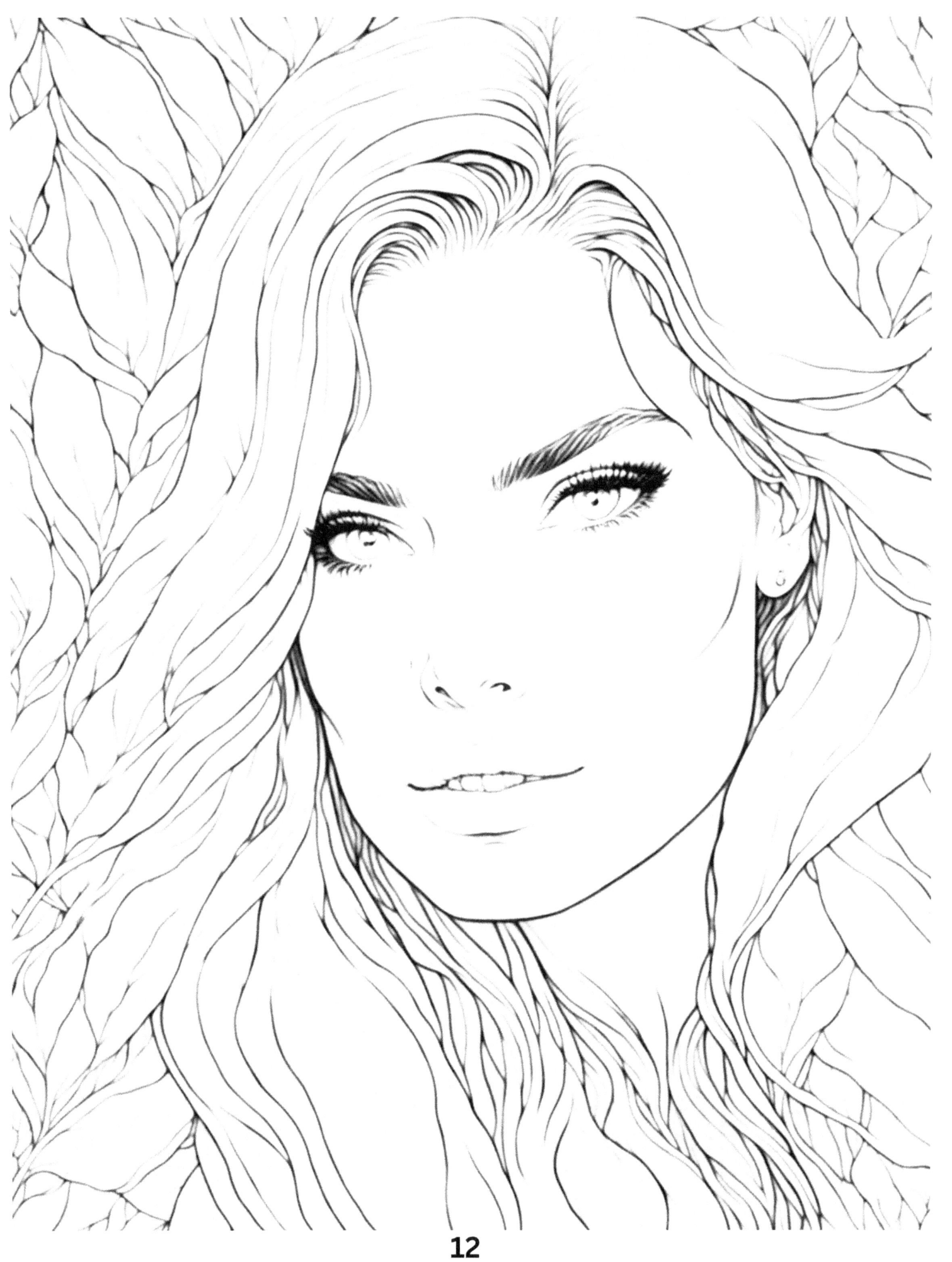

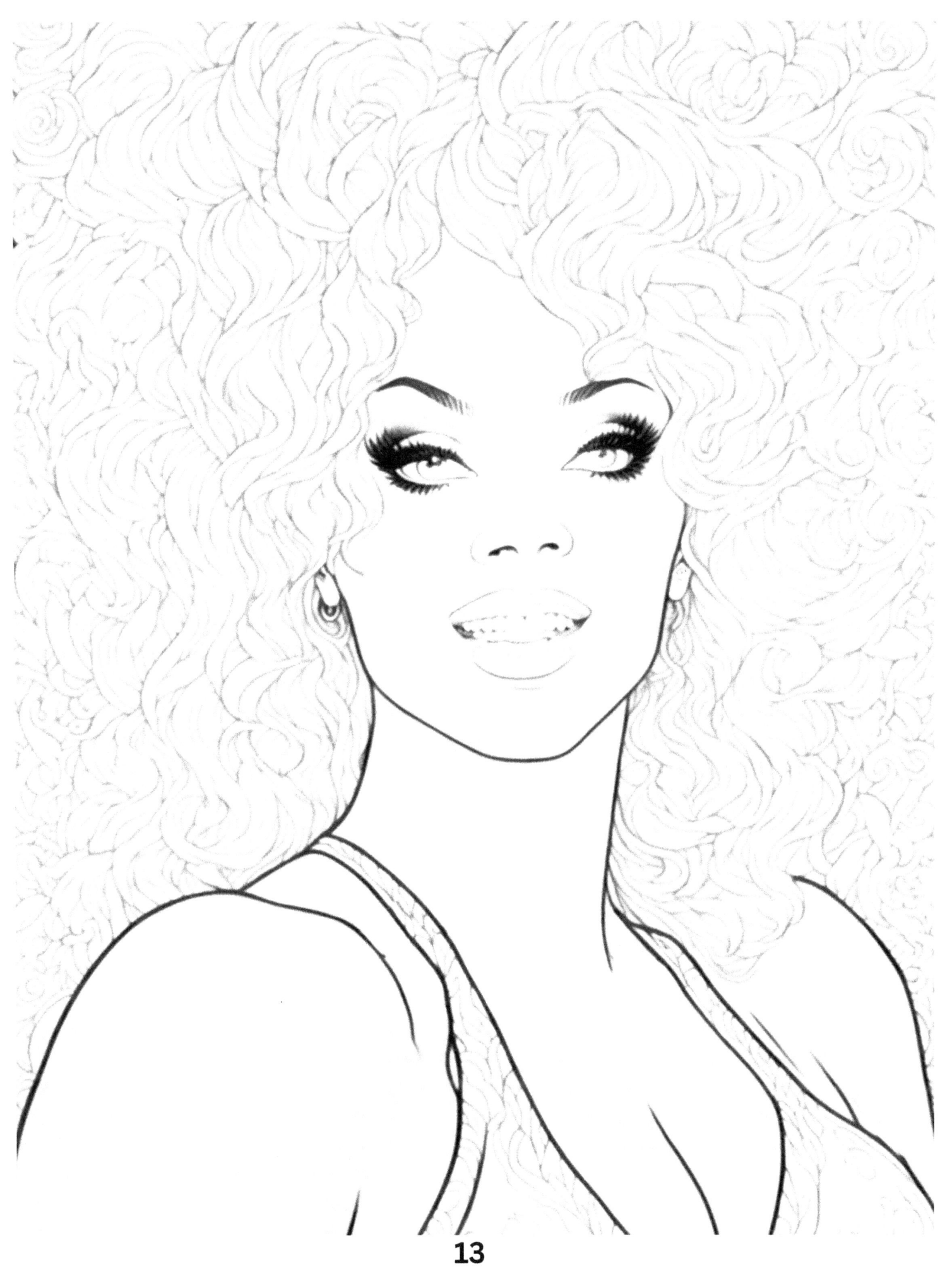

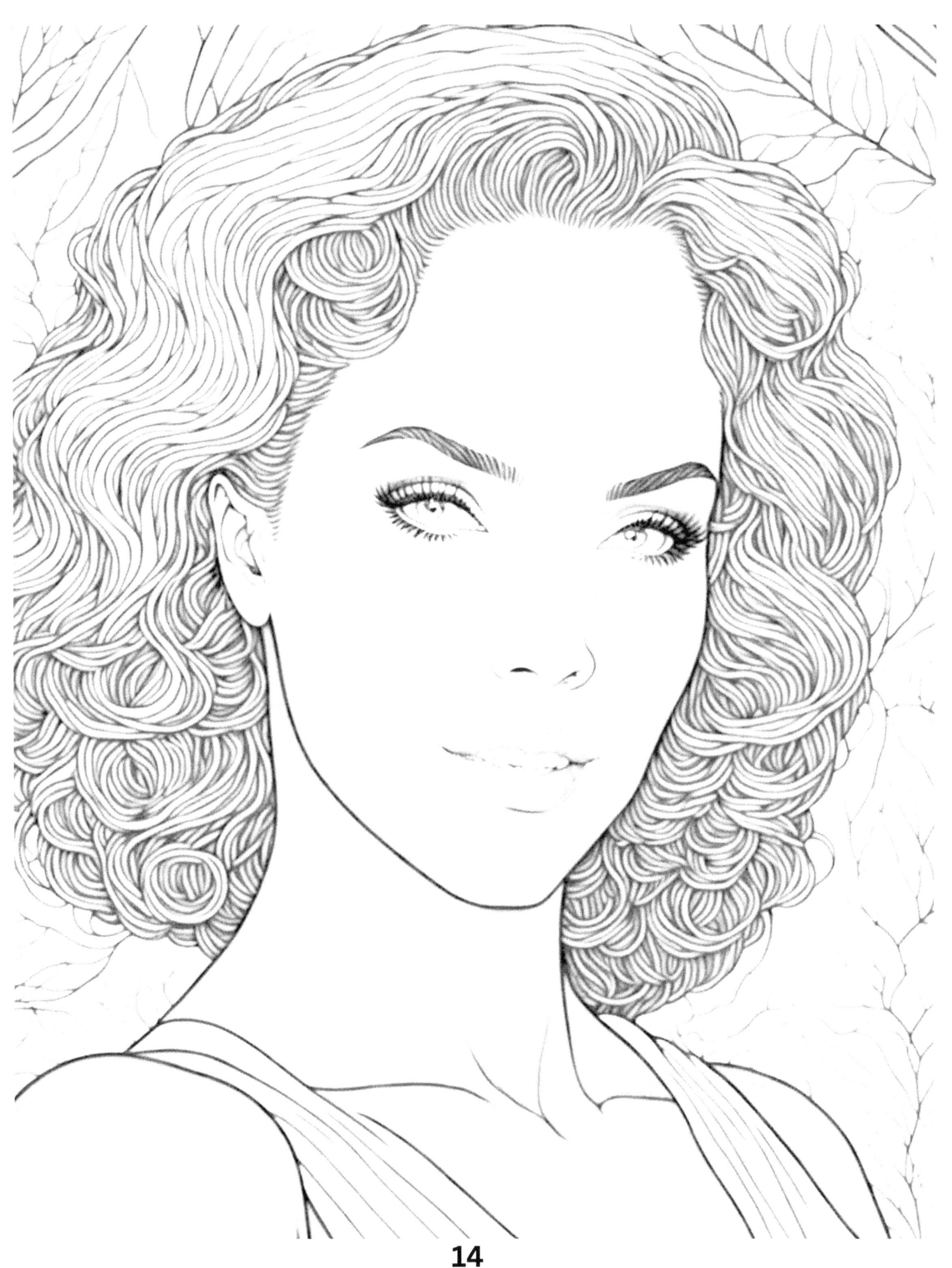

14

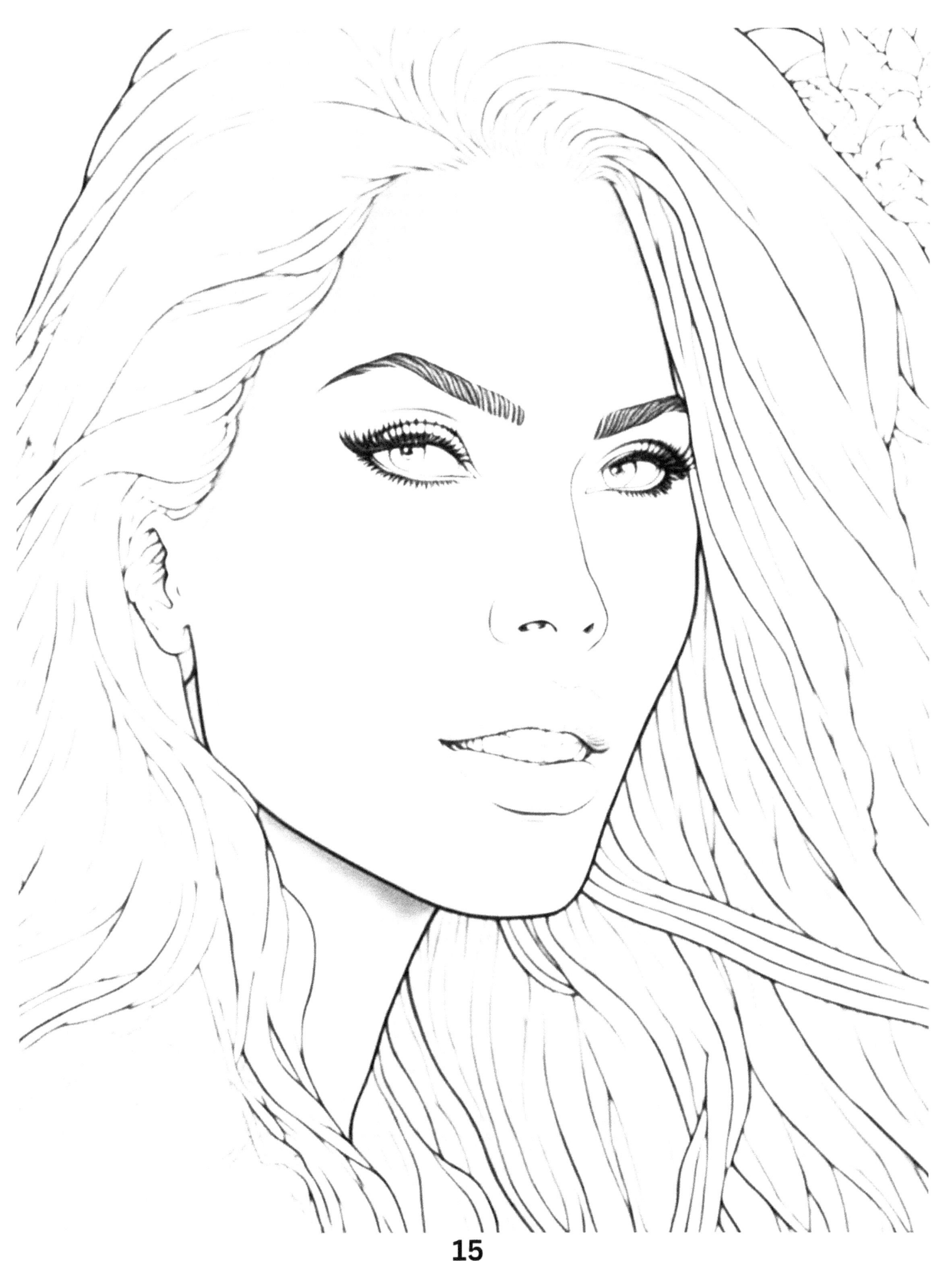

15

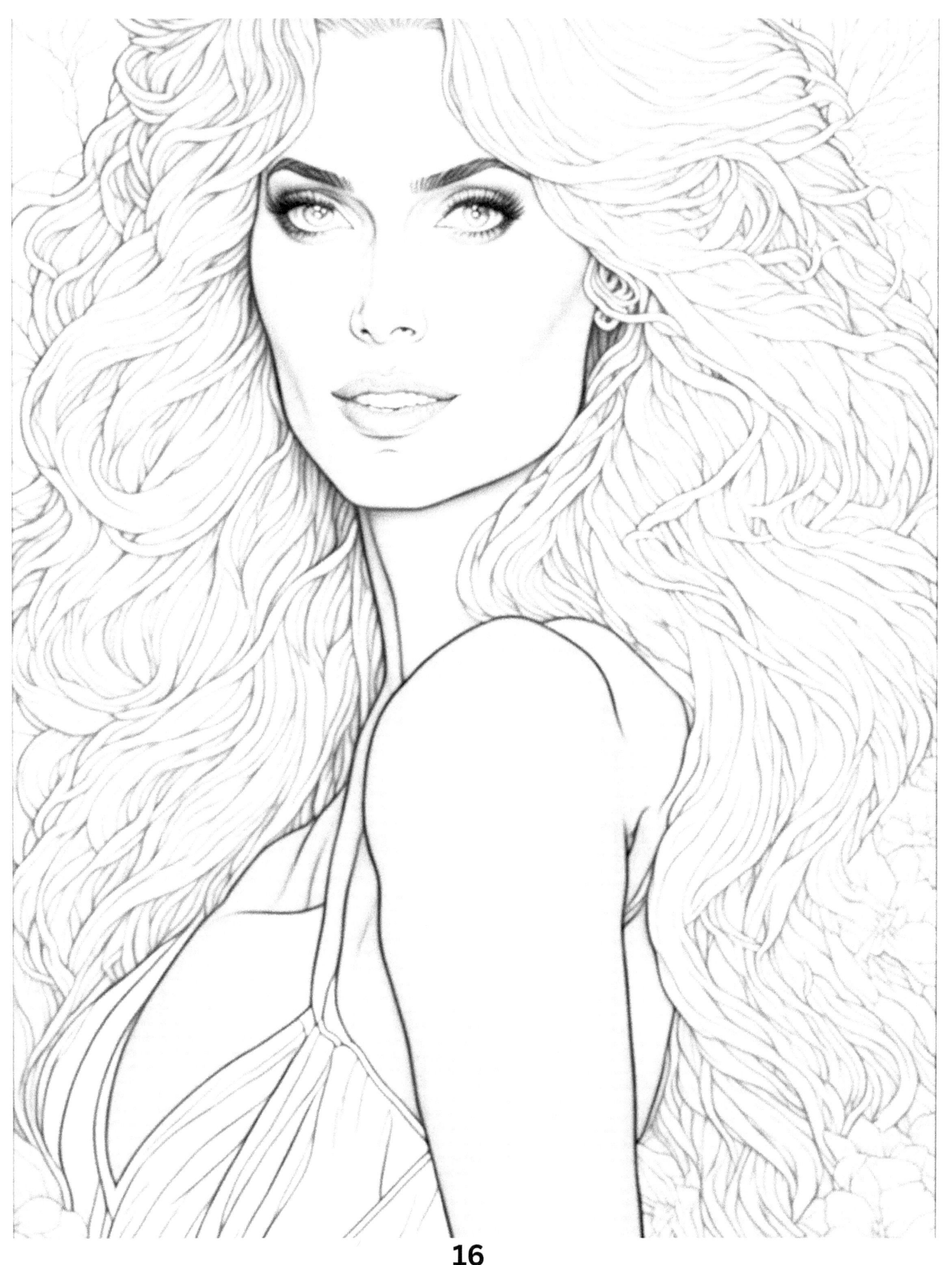

16

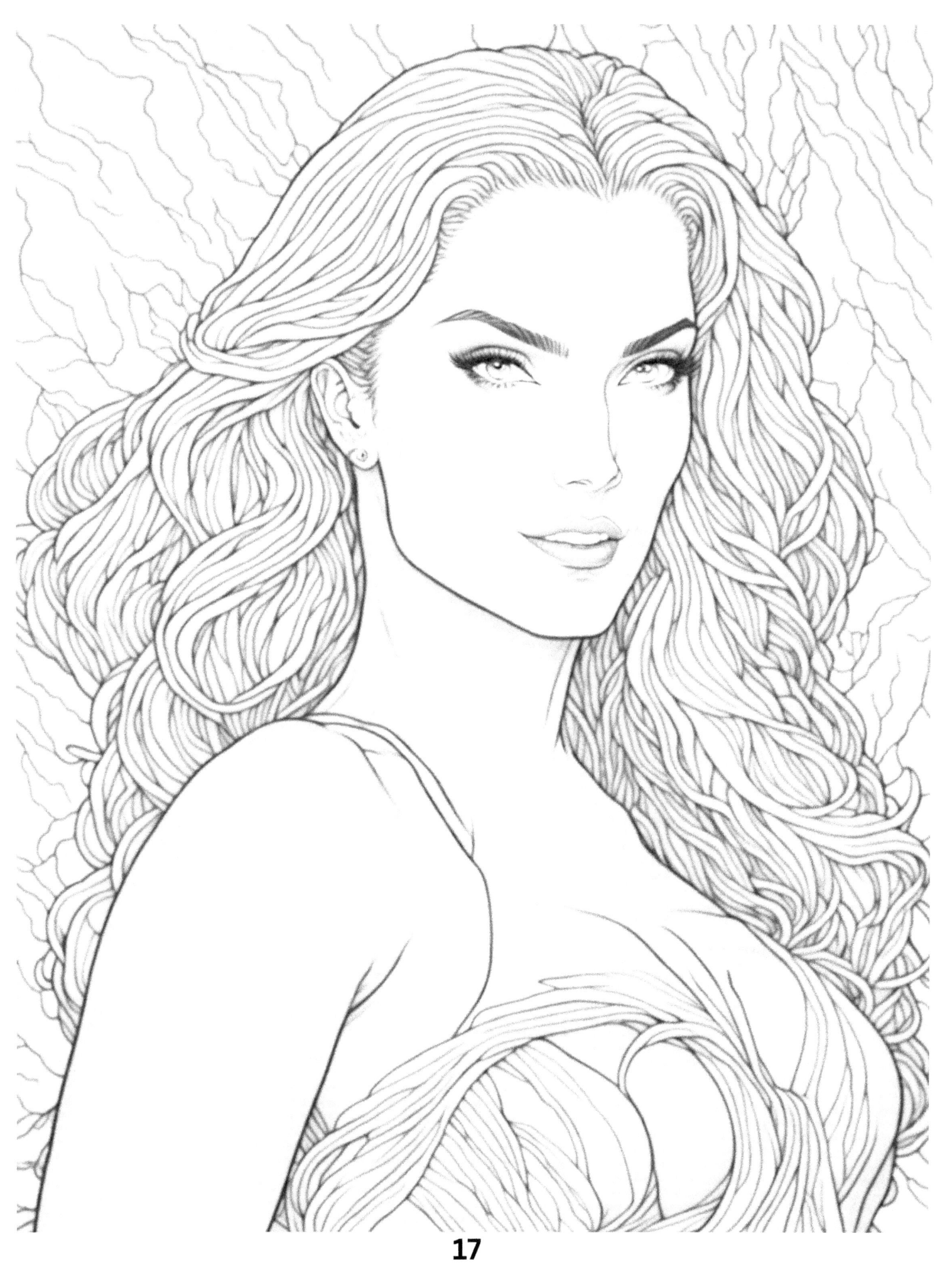

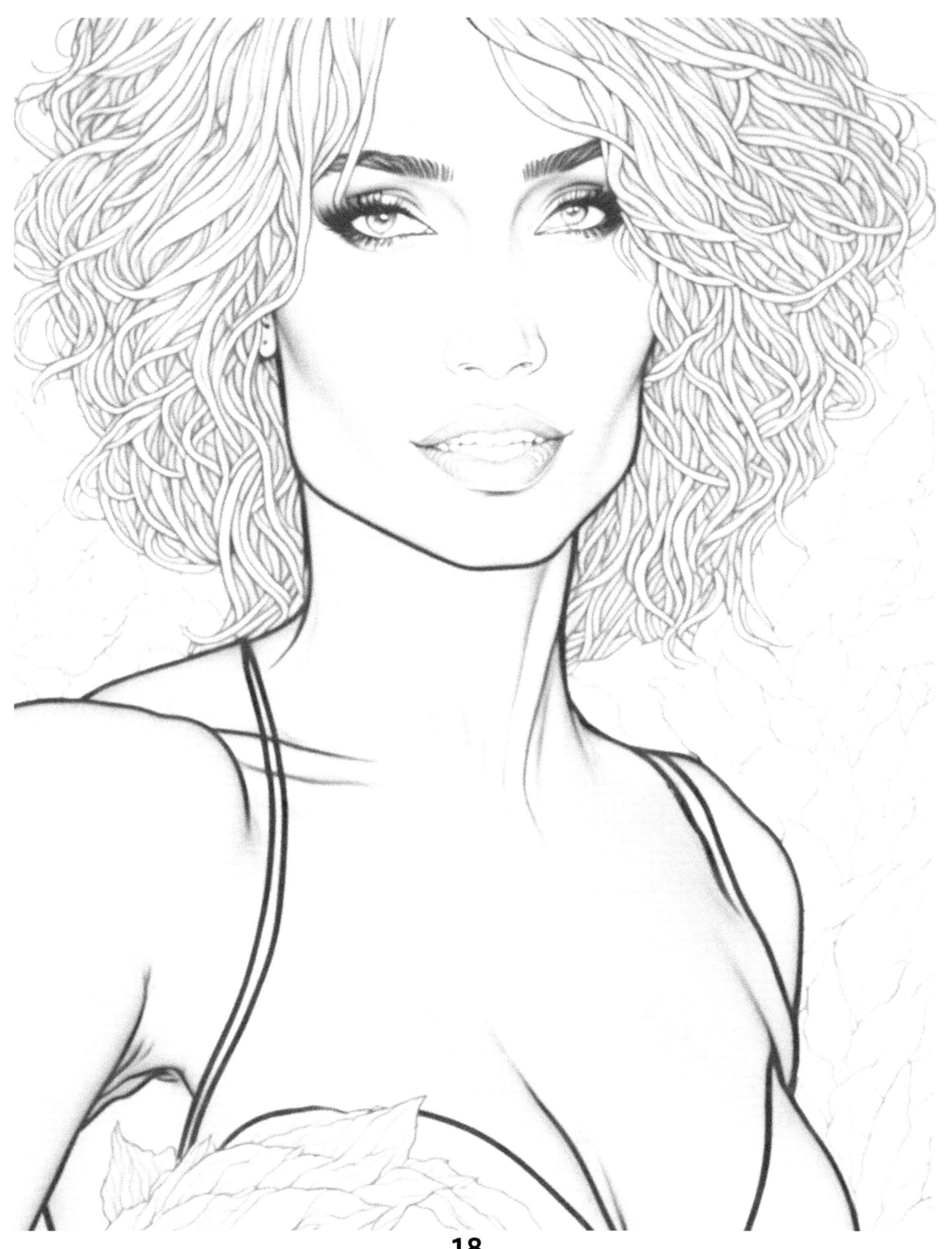

18

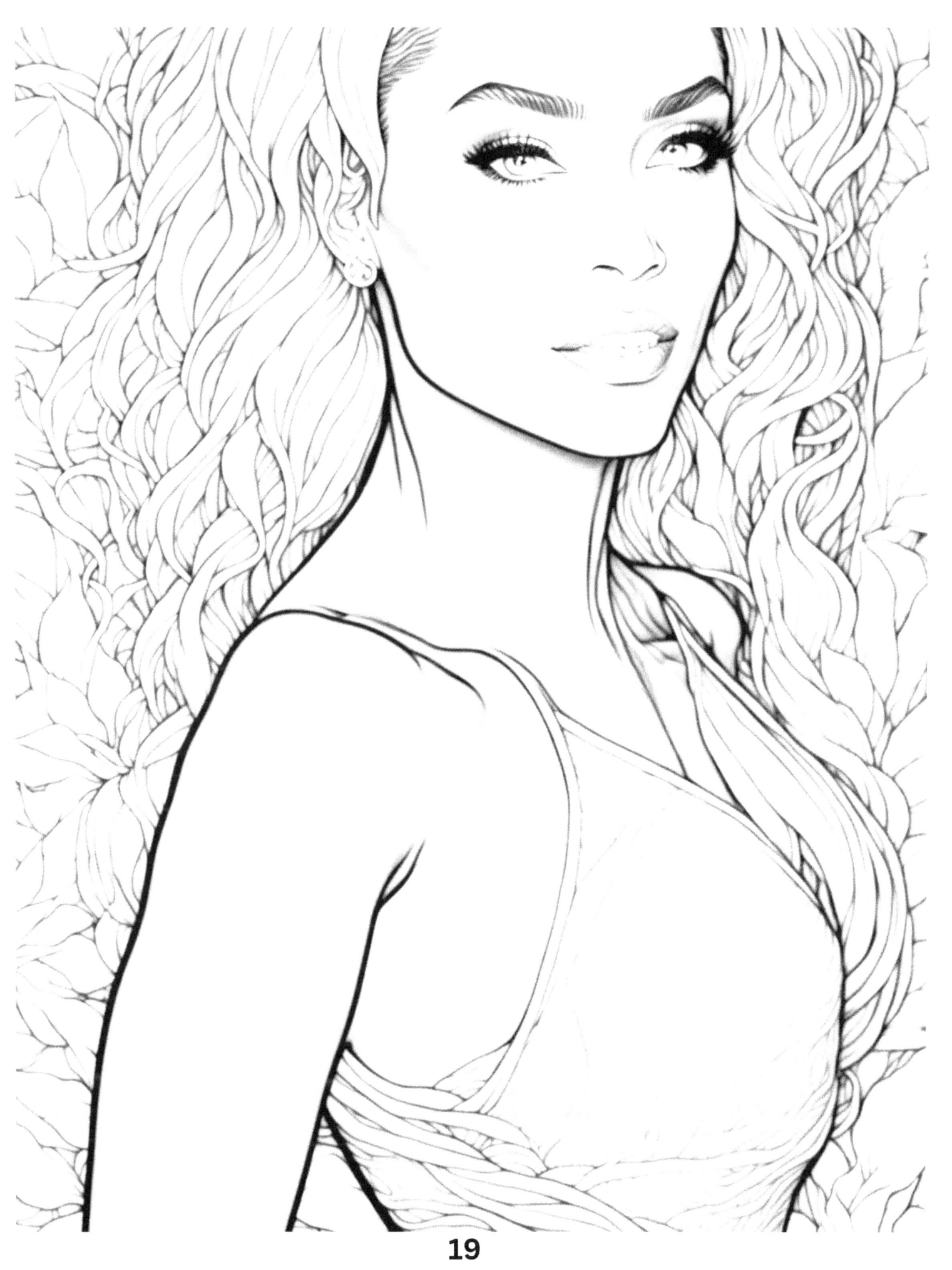

19

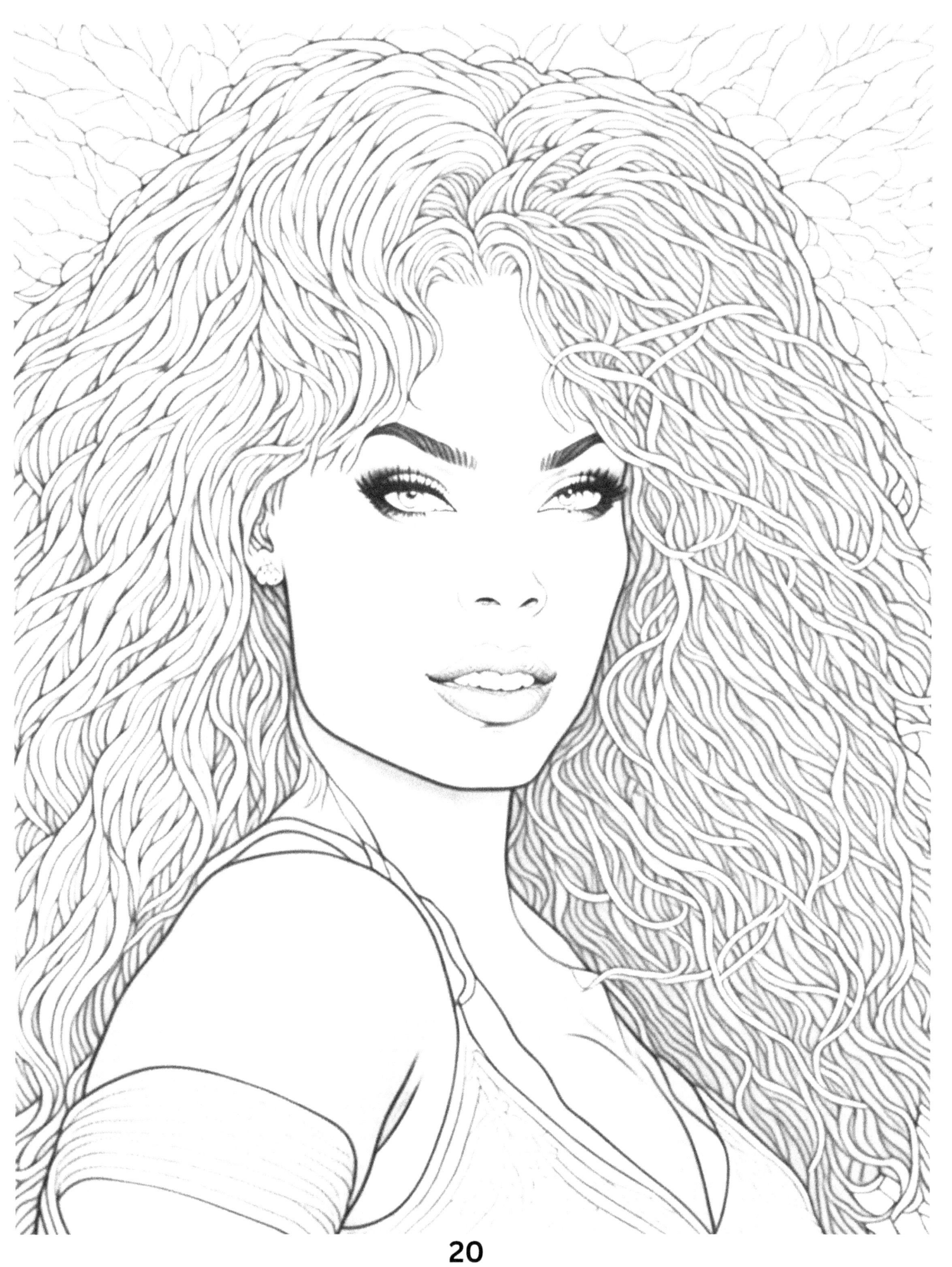

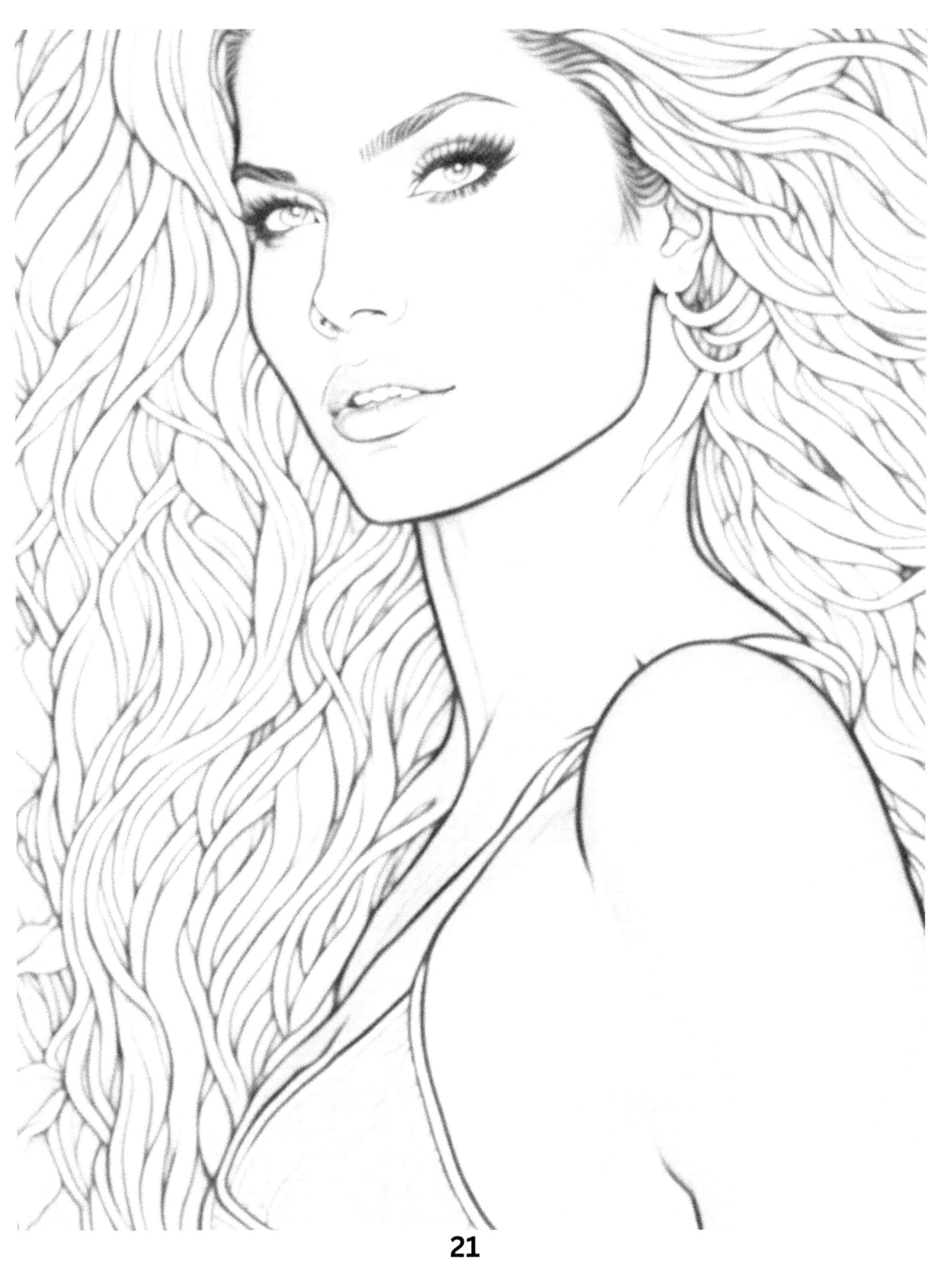

21

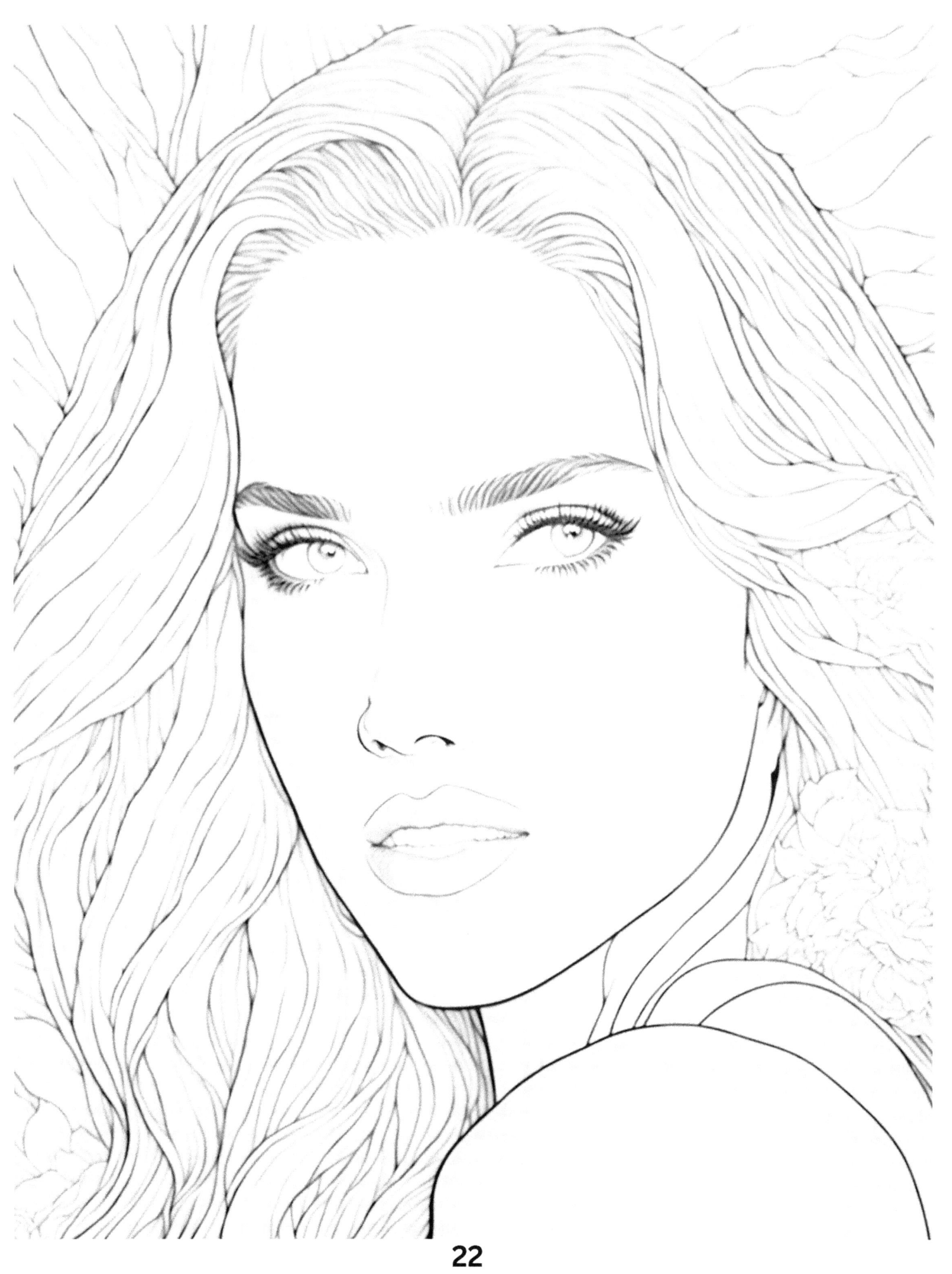

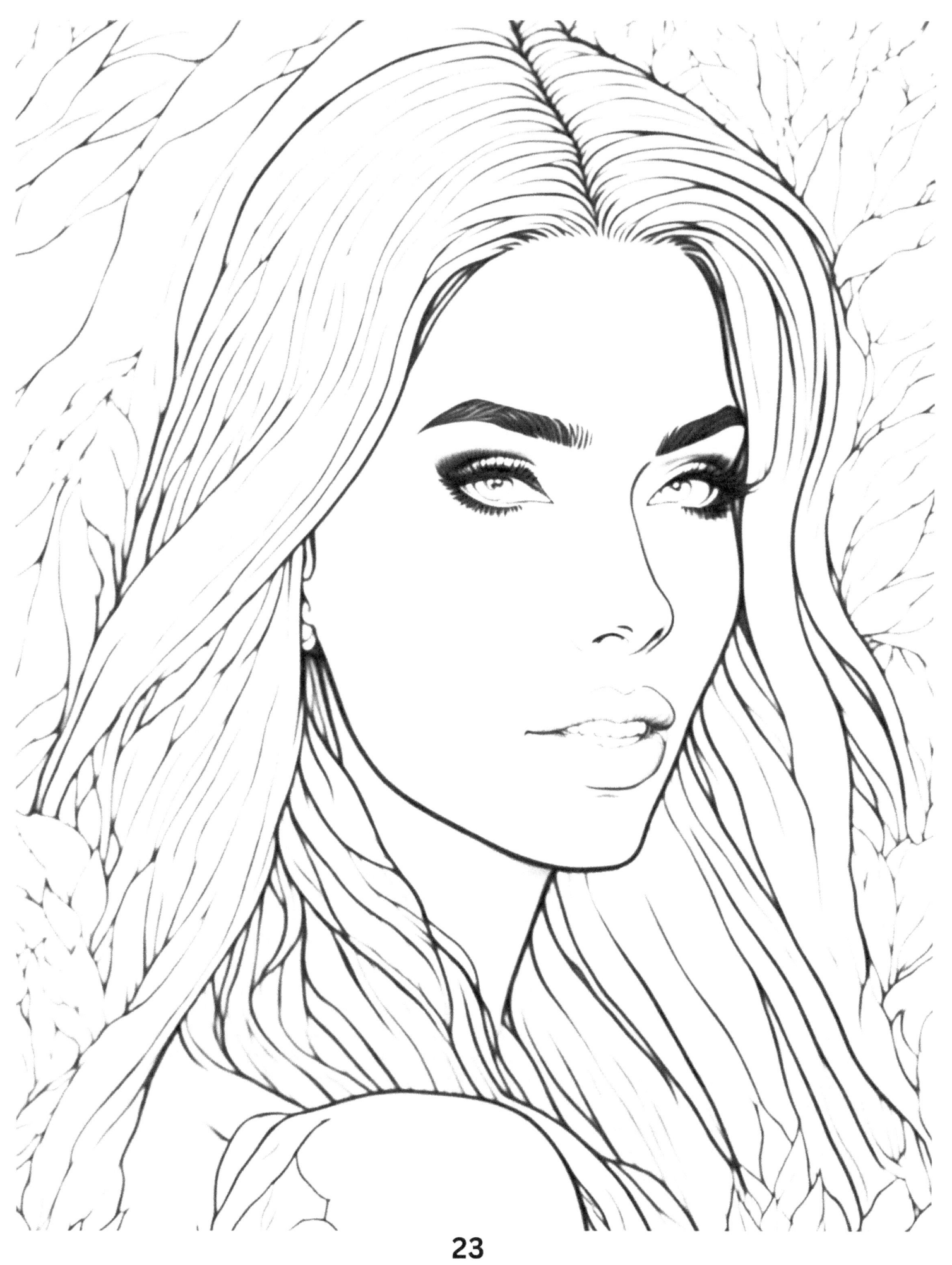

23

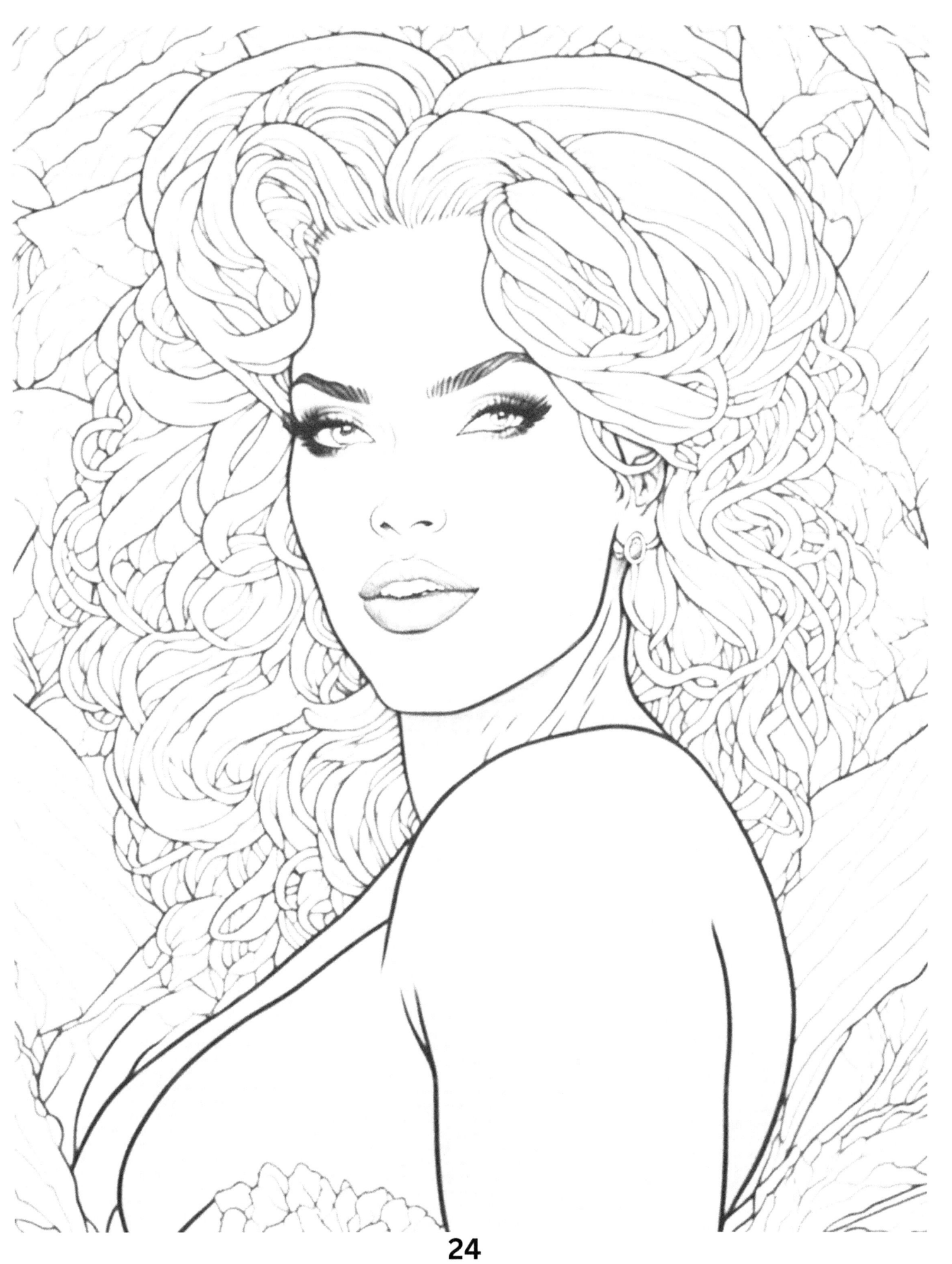

24

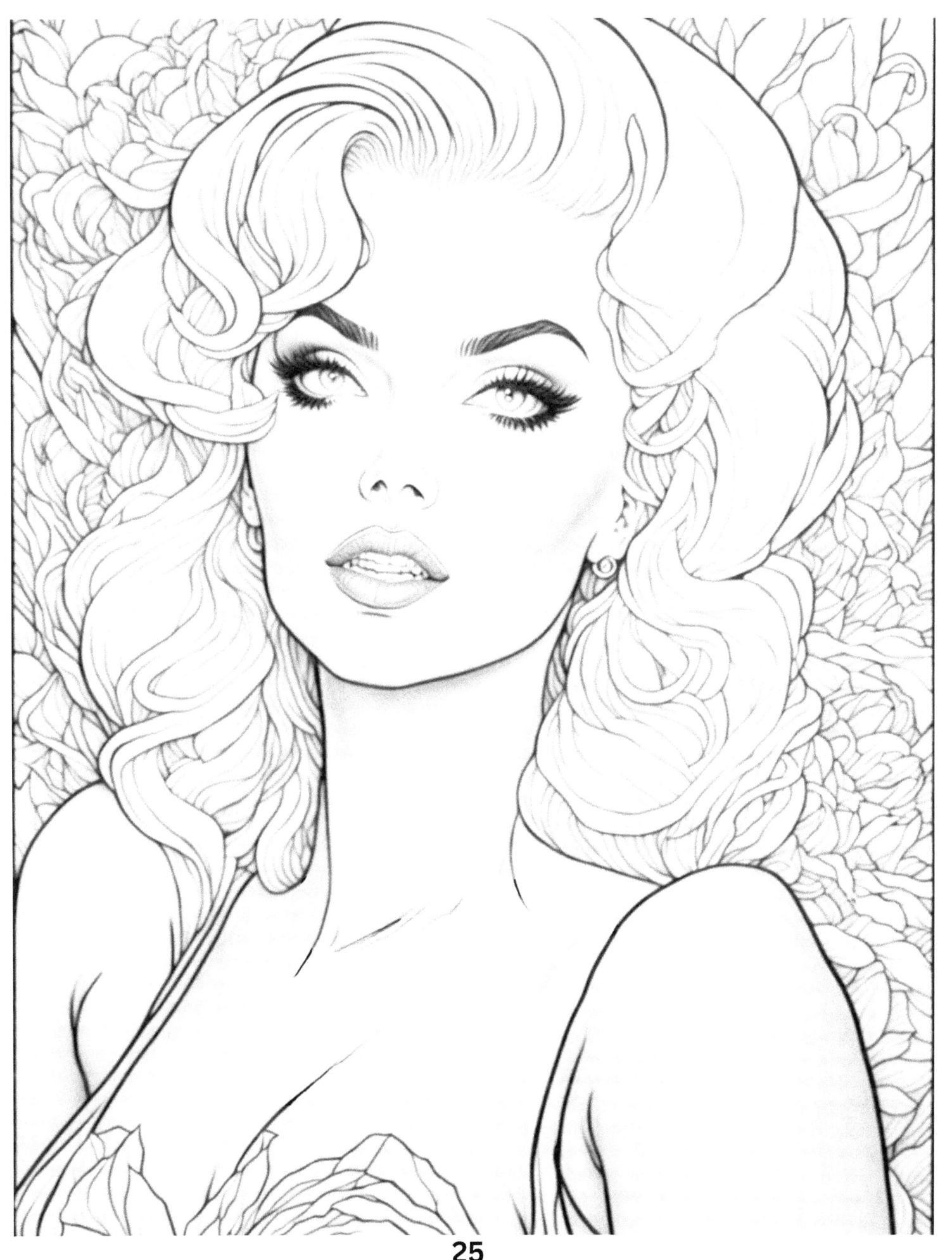

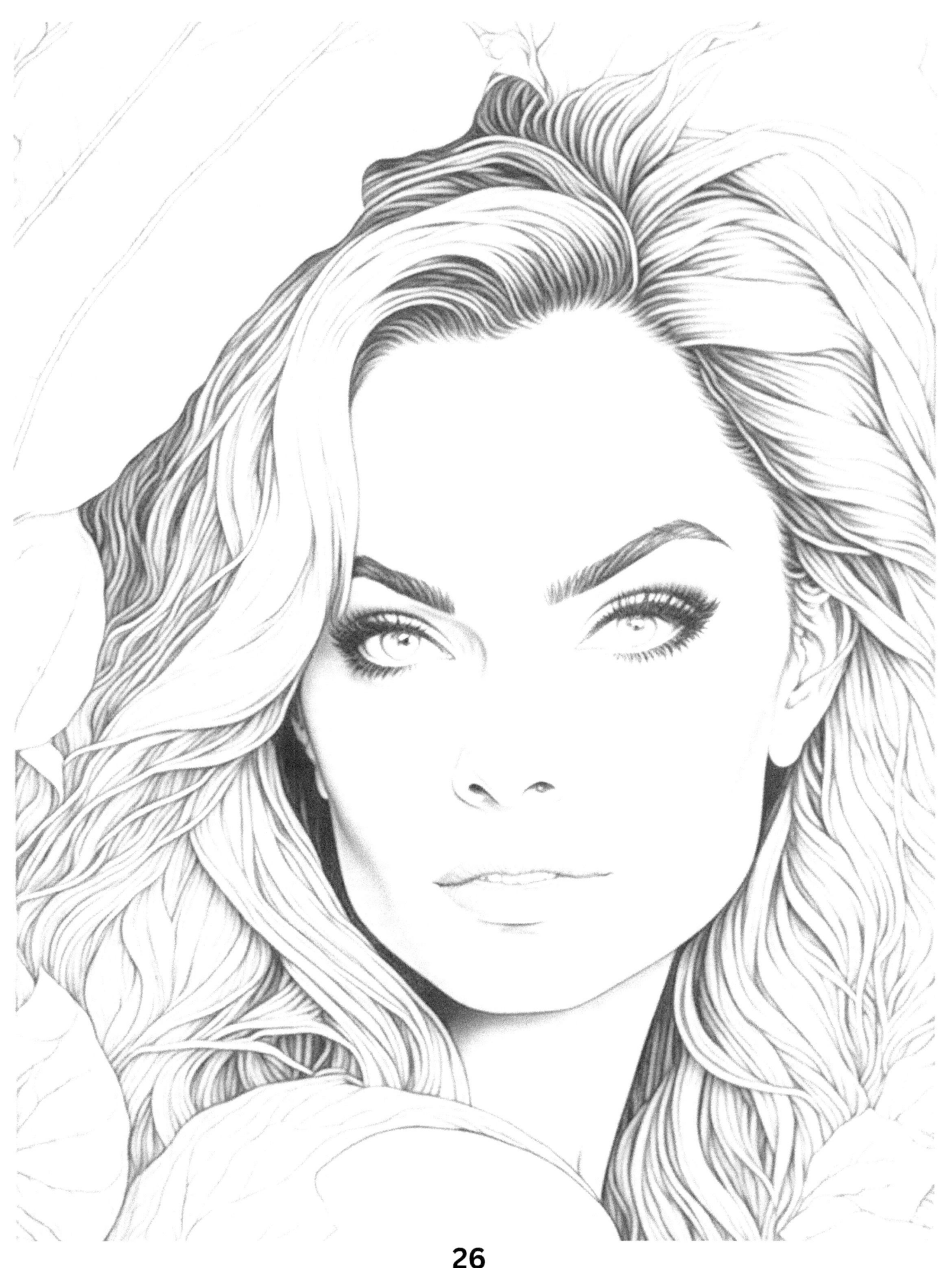

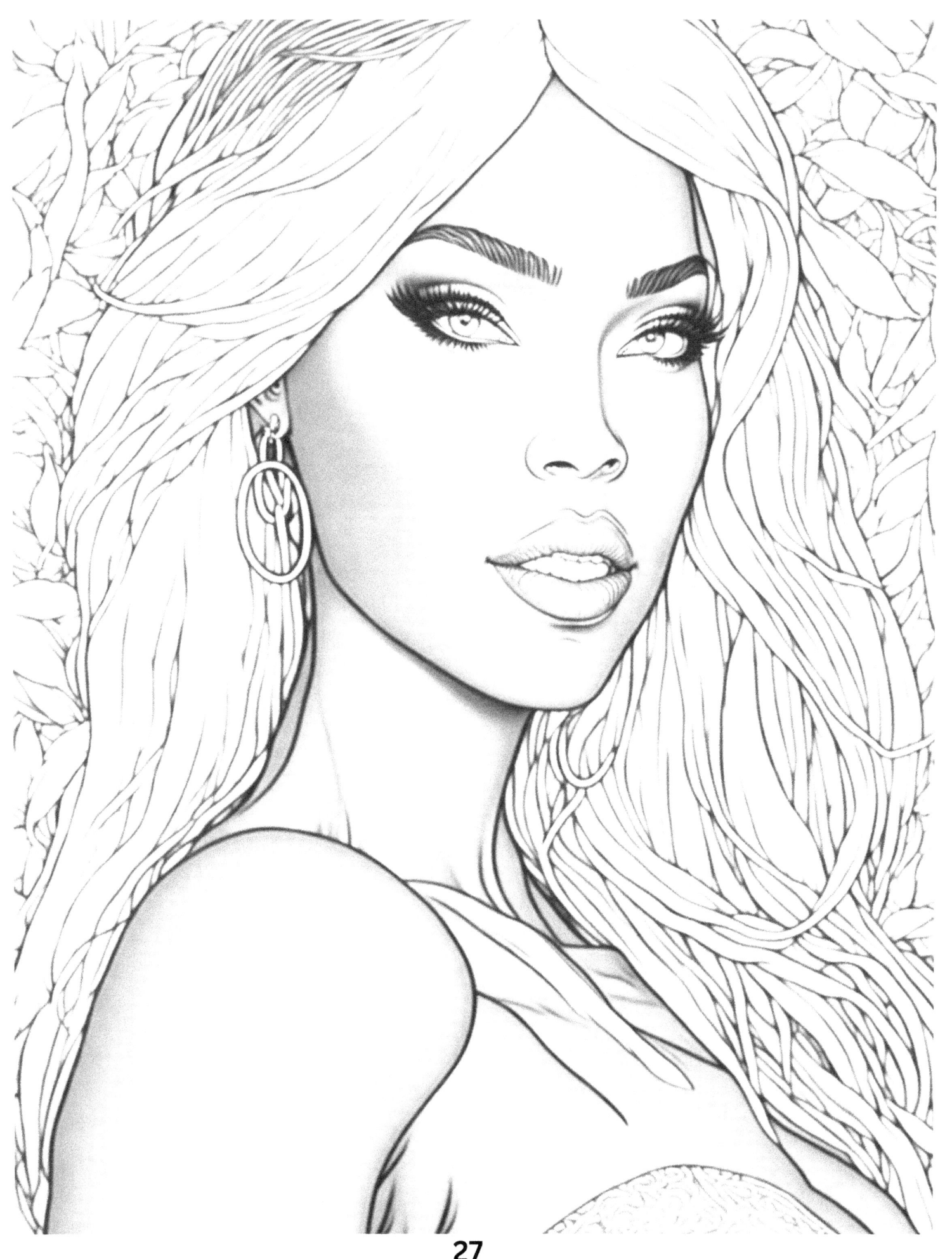

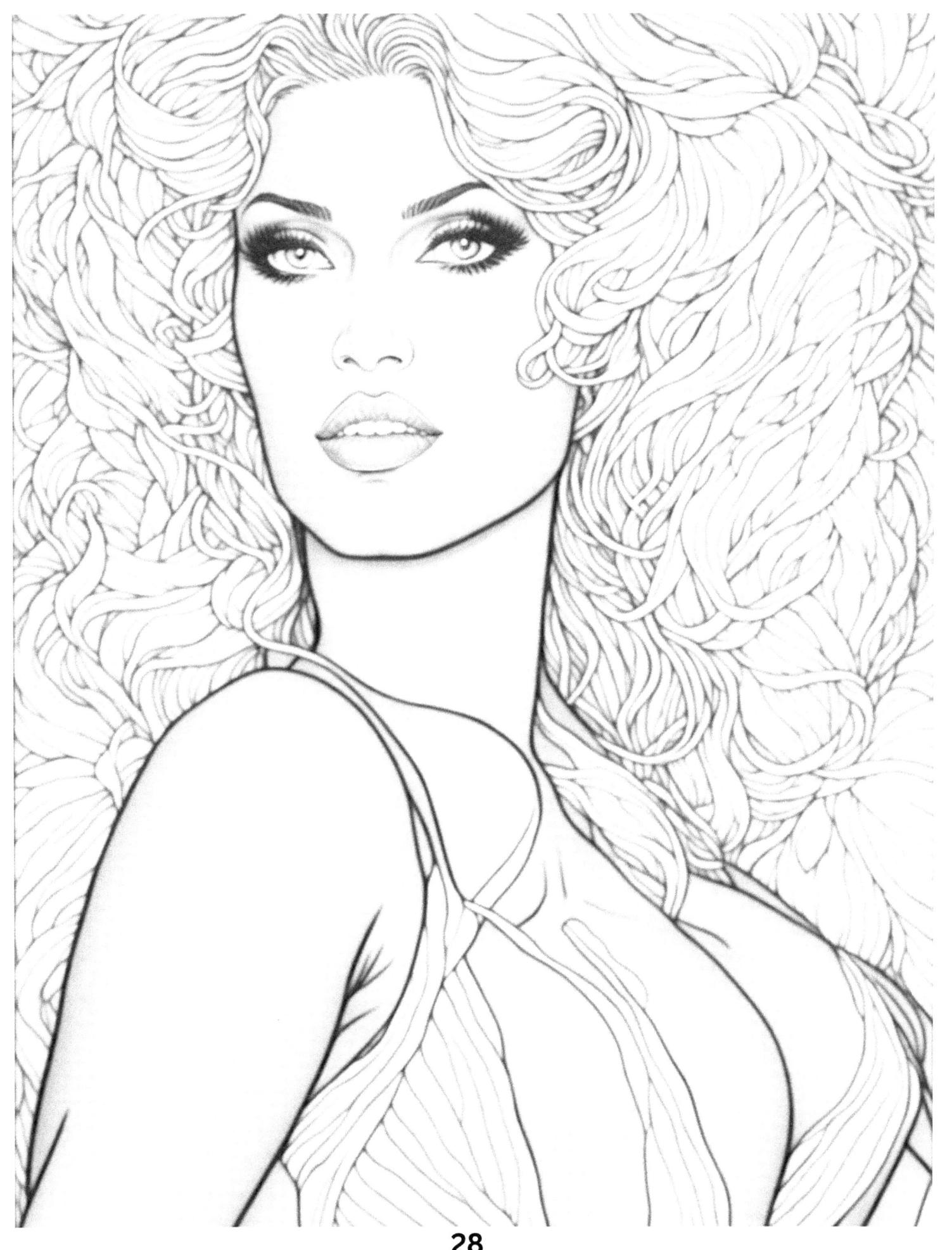

28

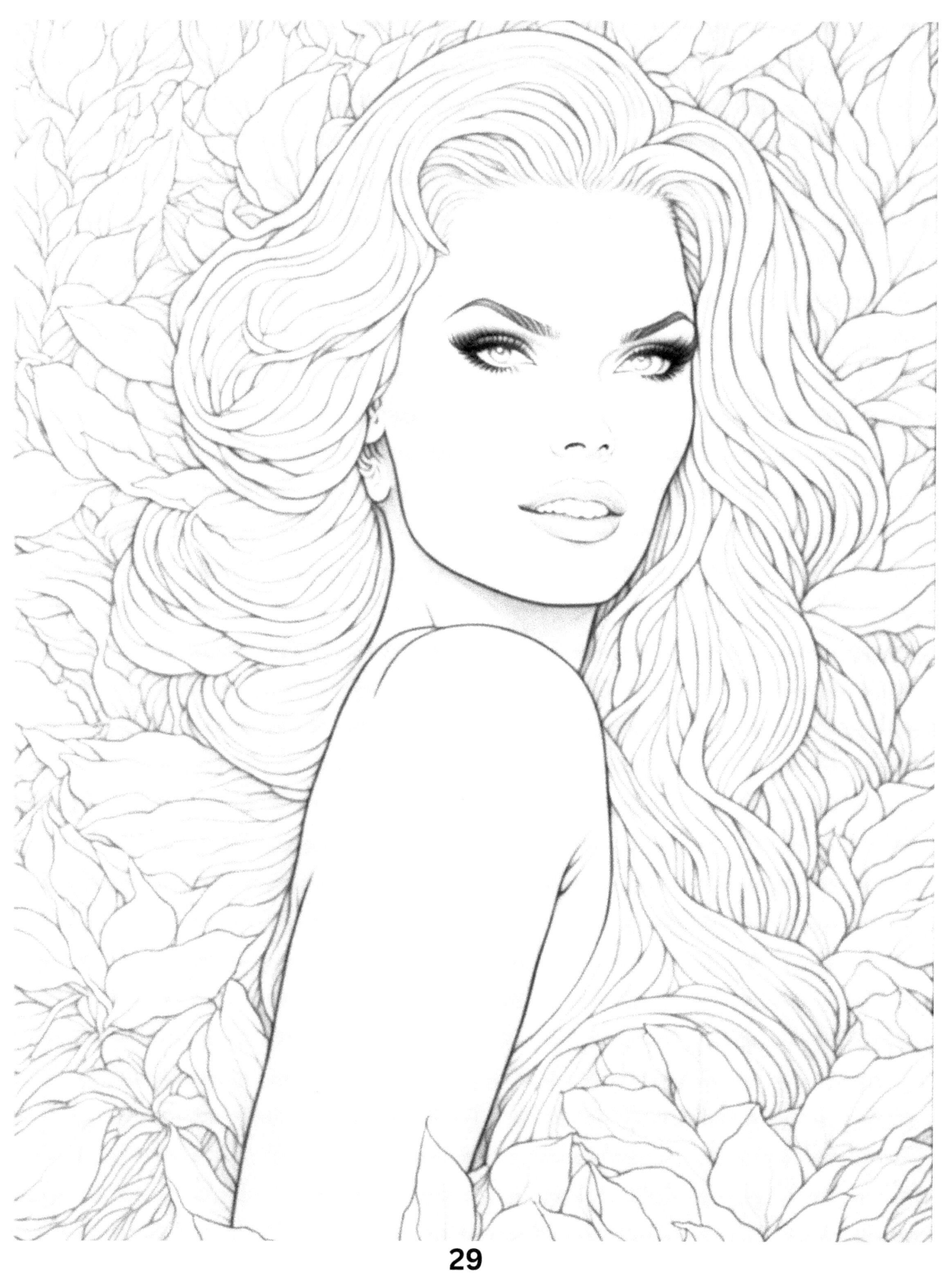

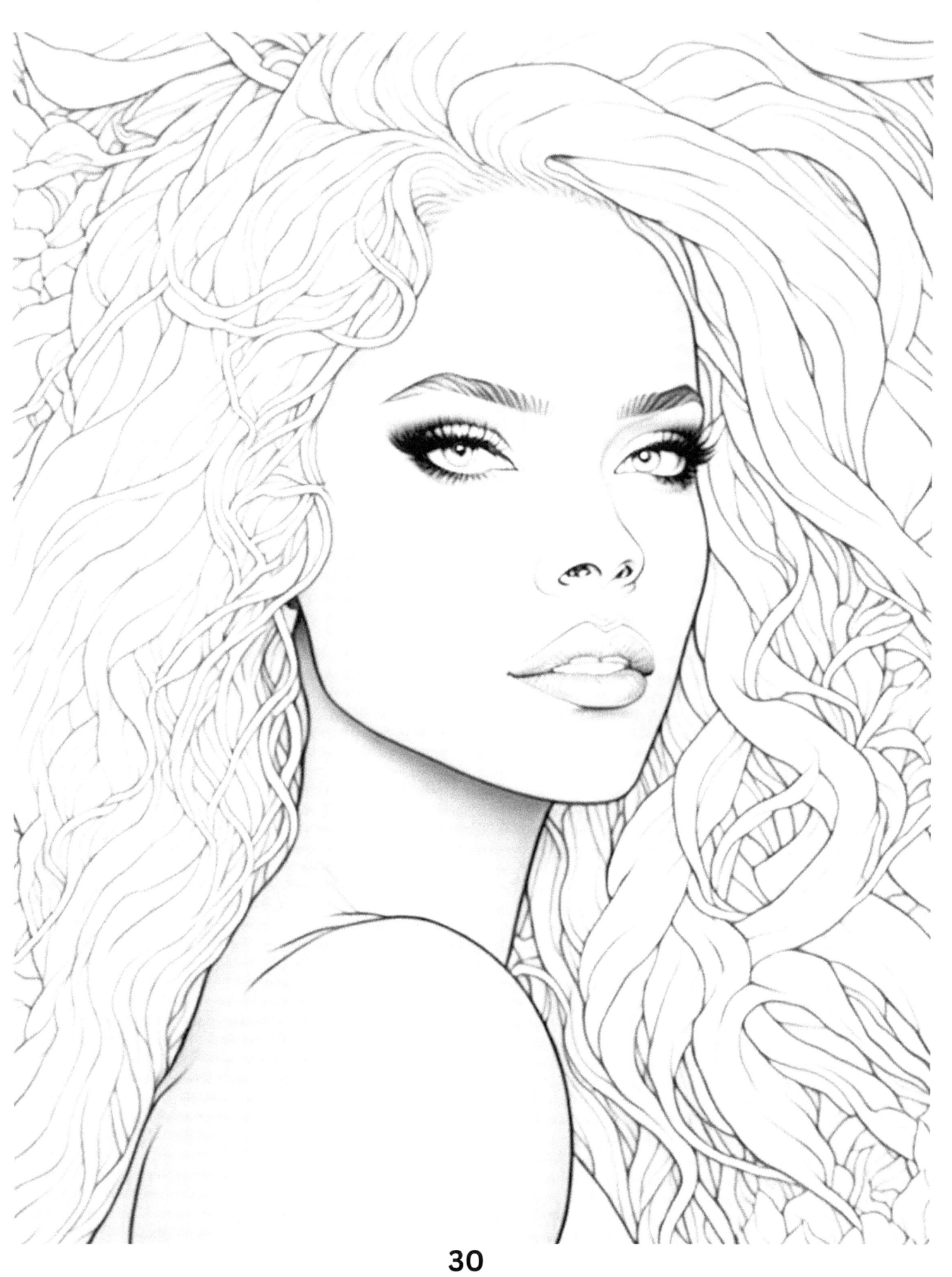

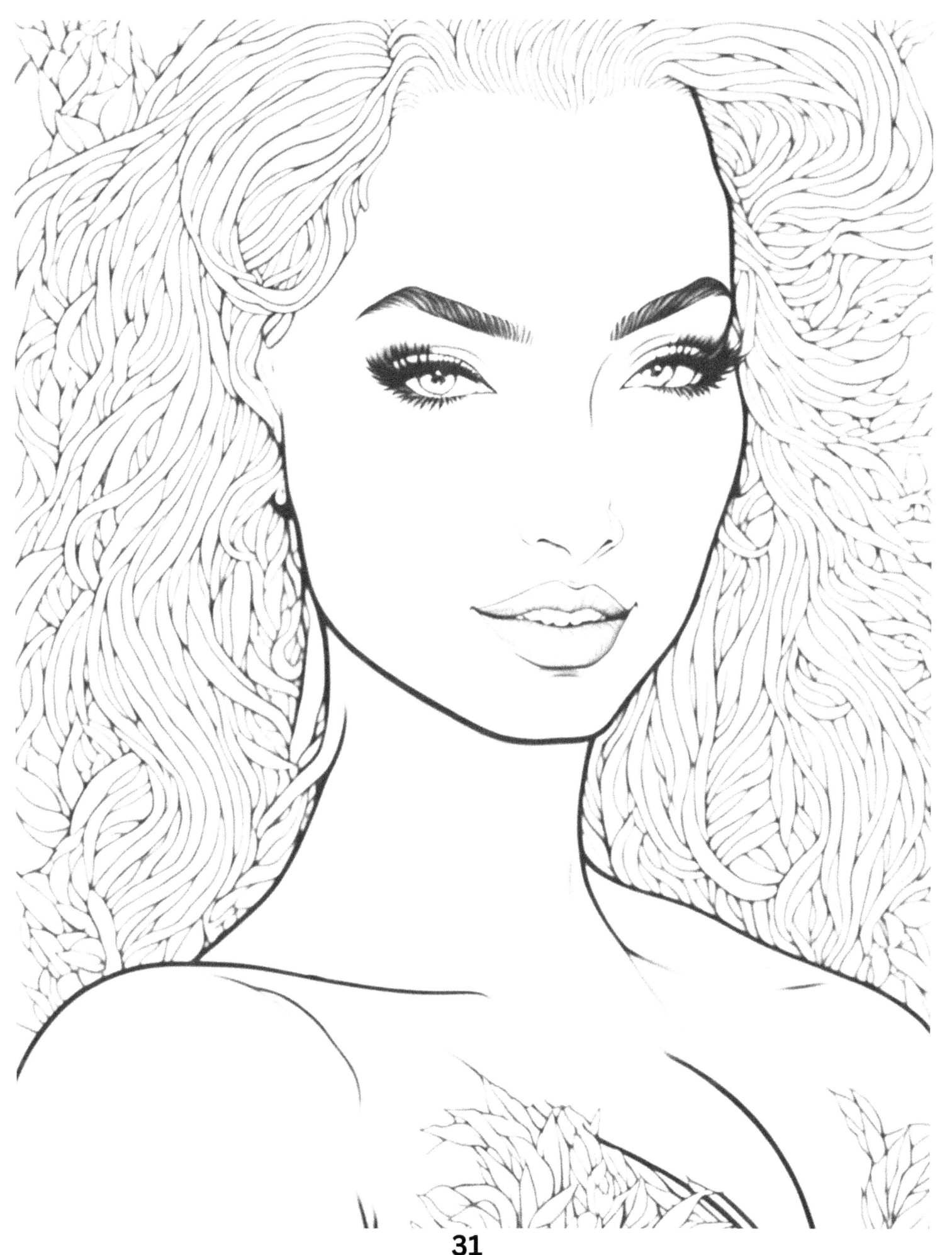

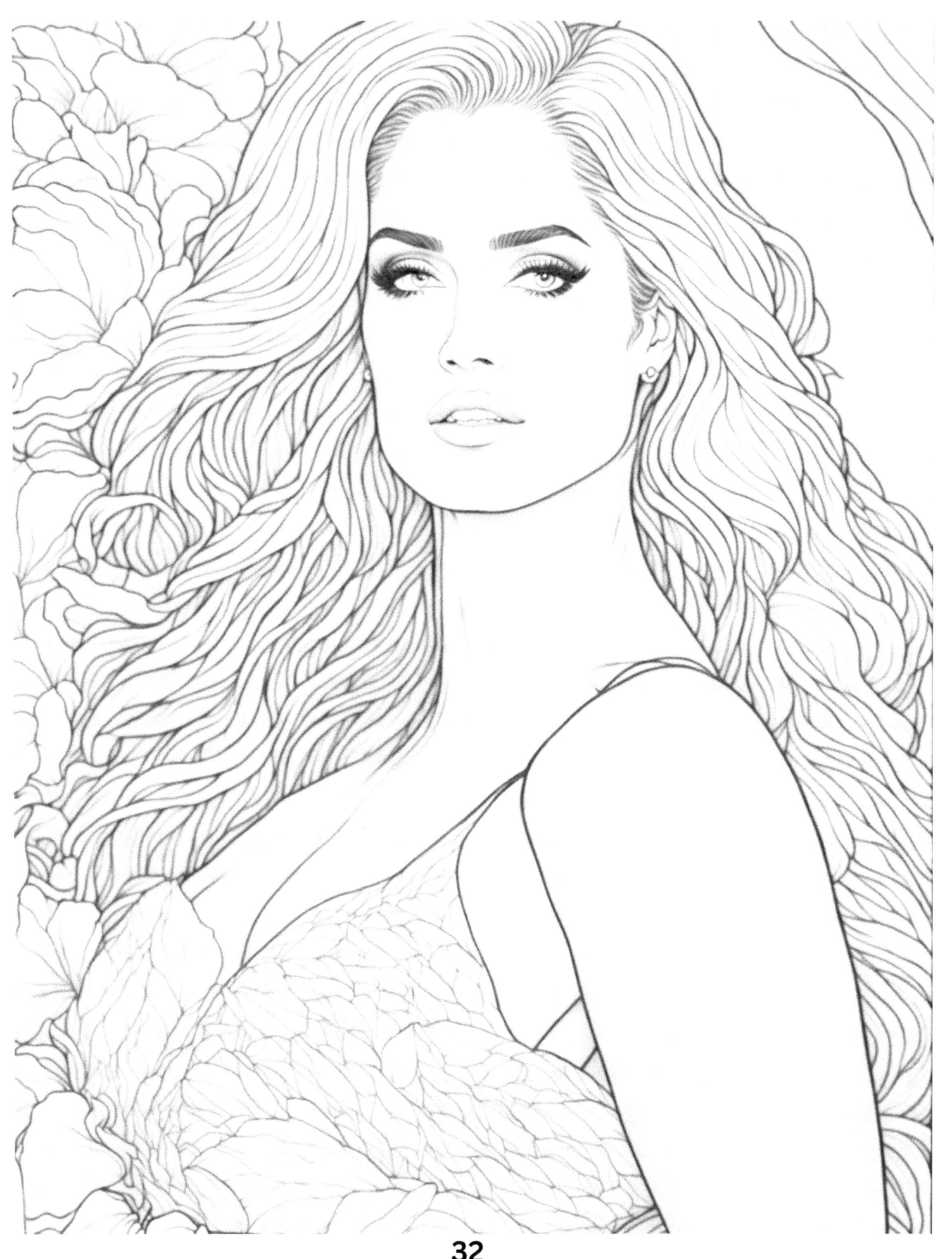

32

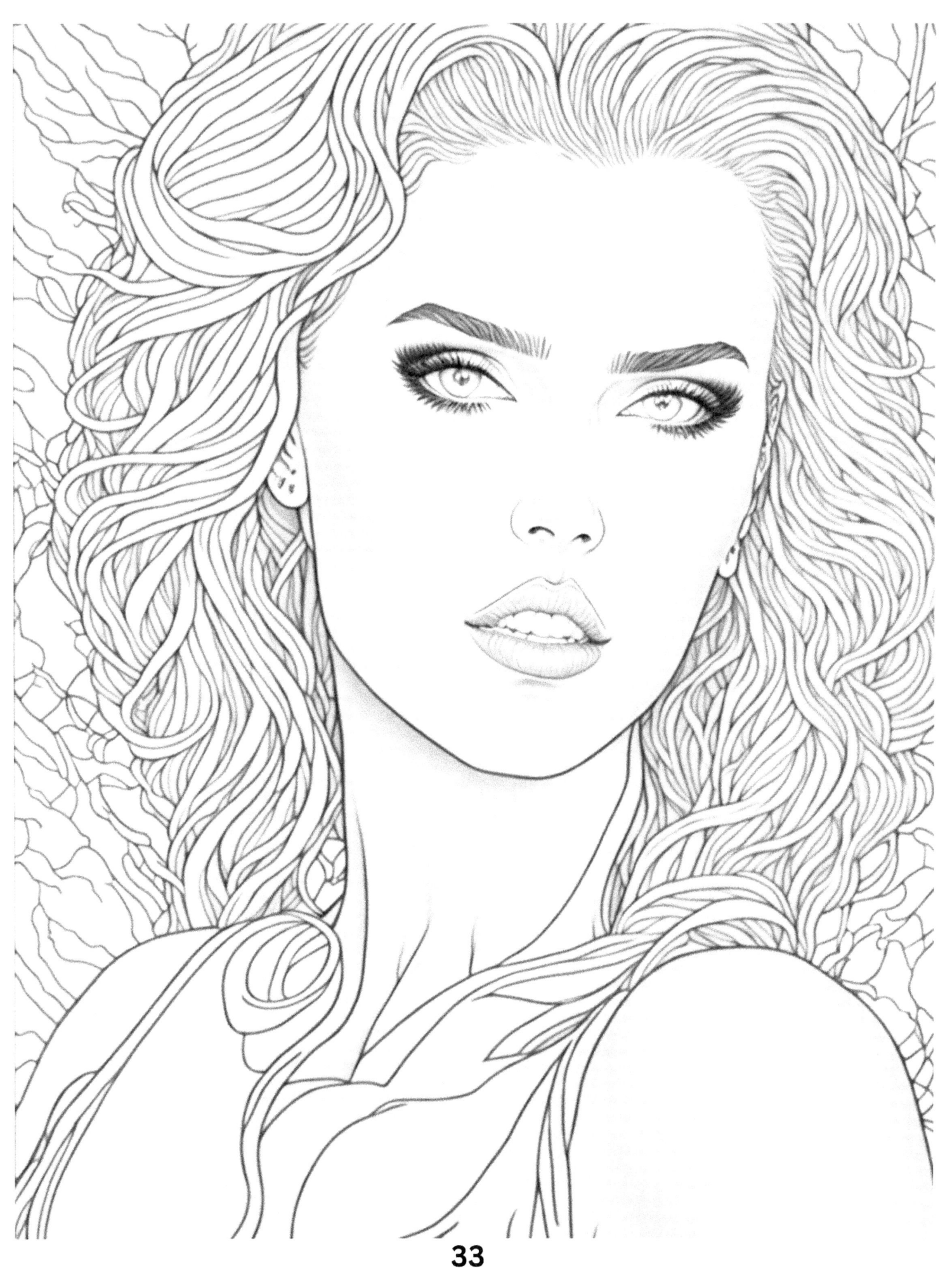

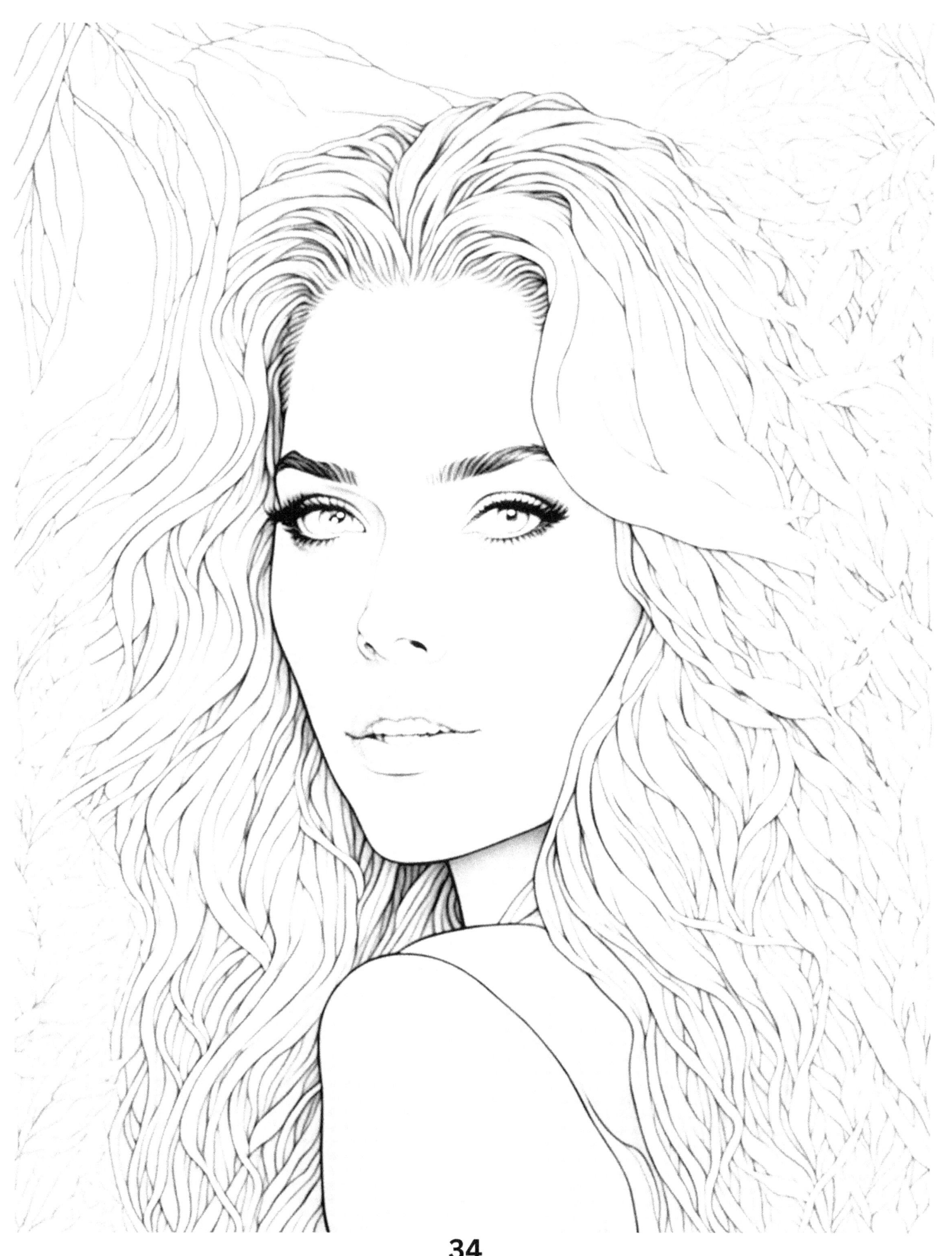

34

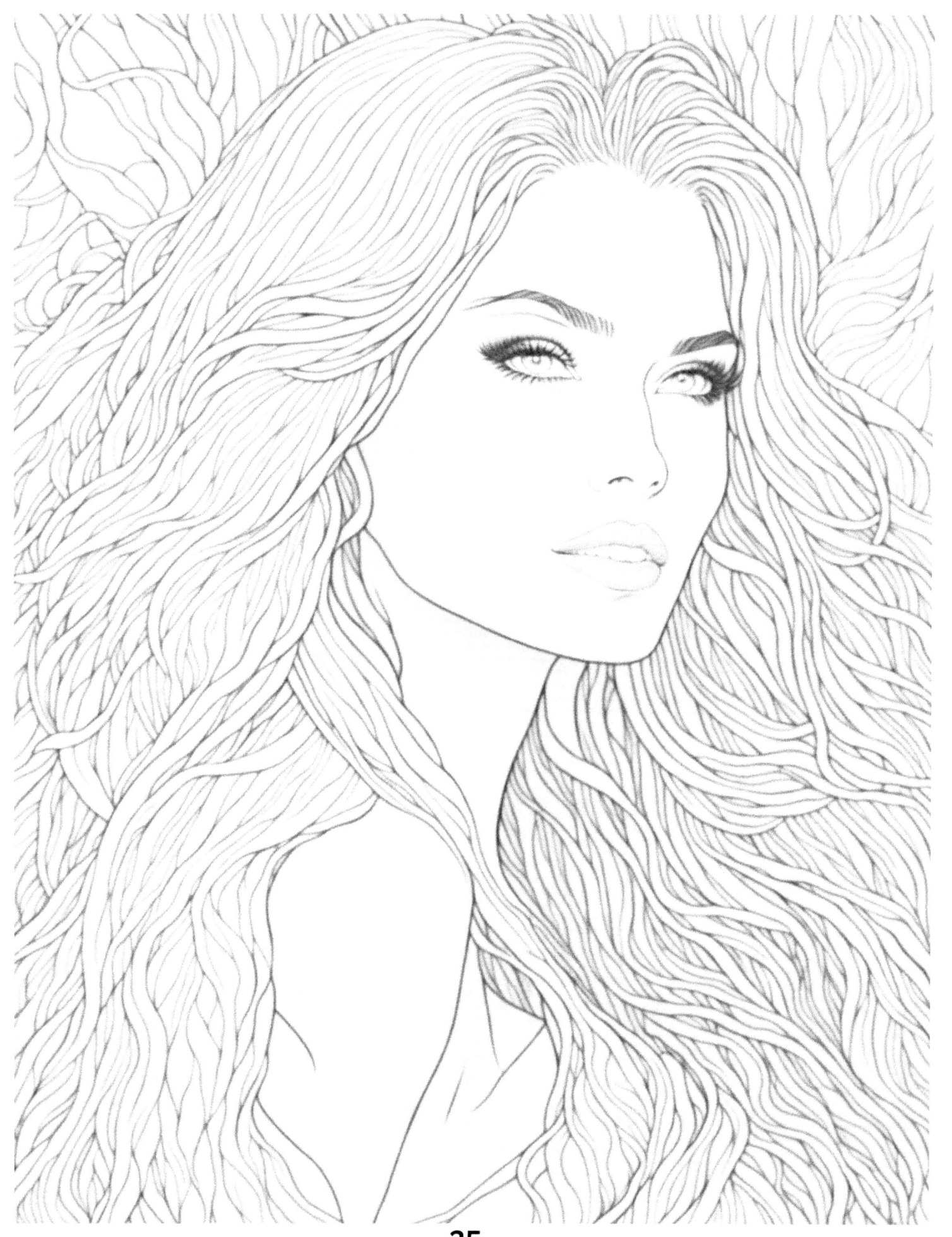

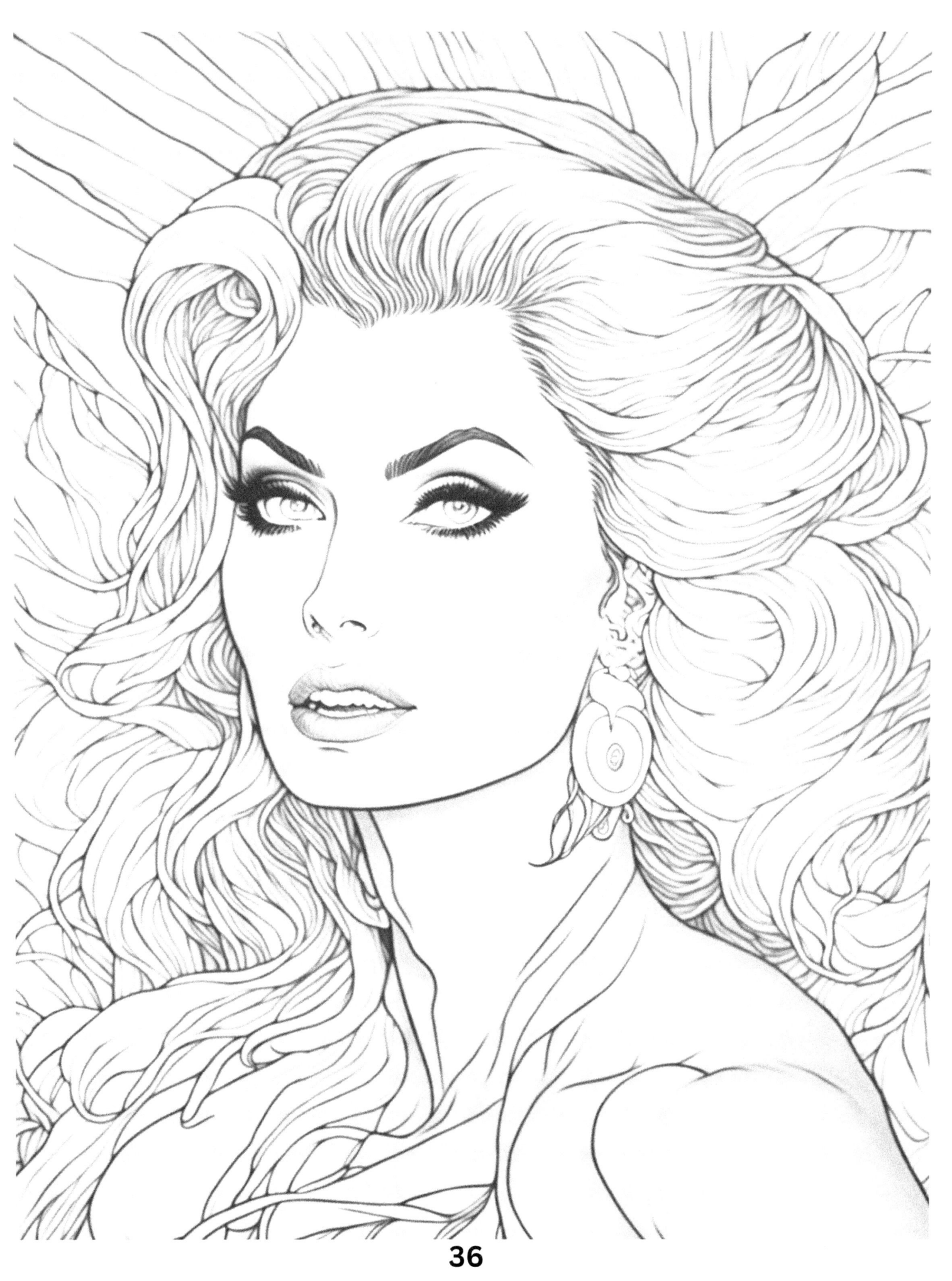

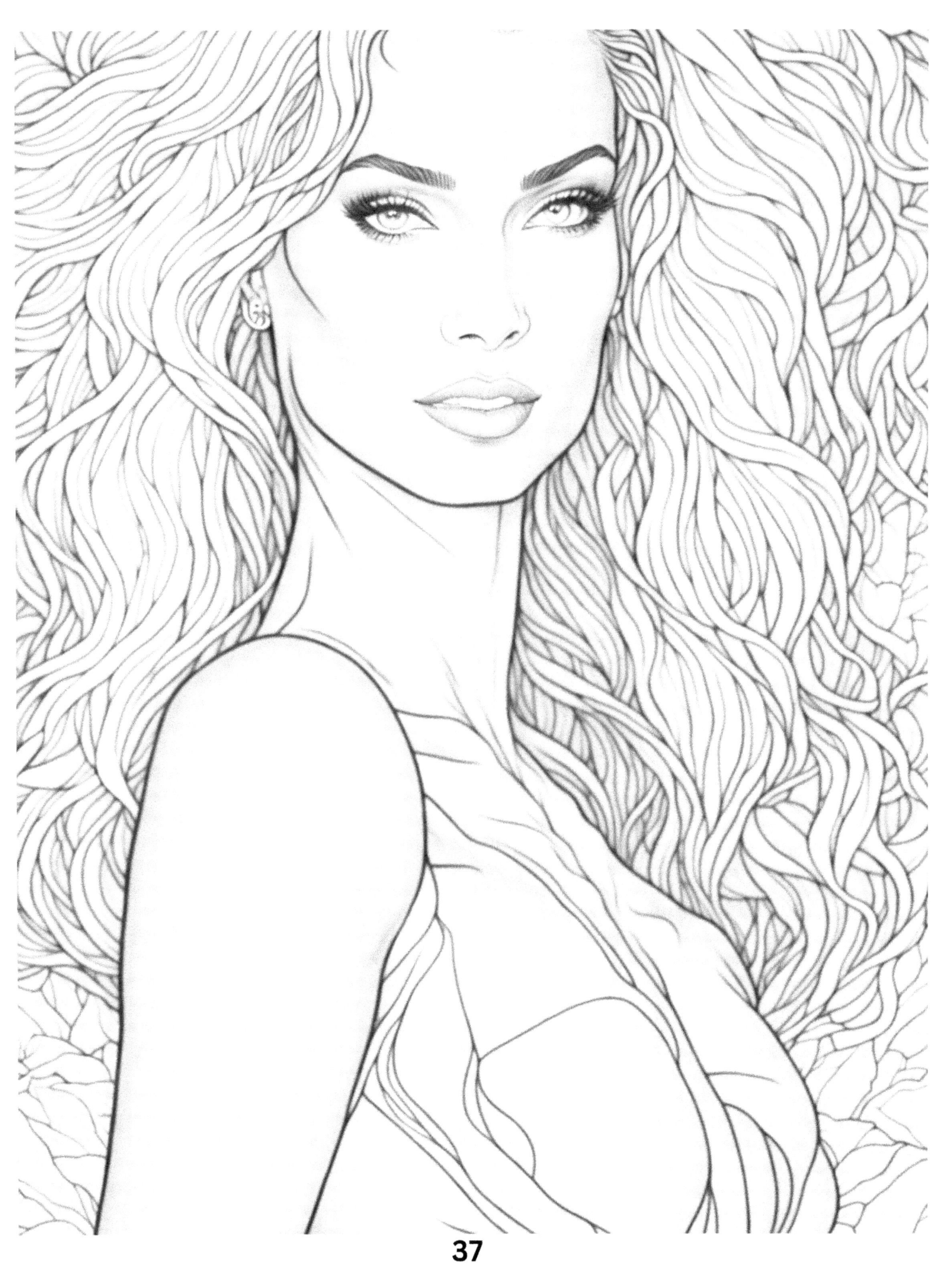

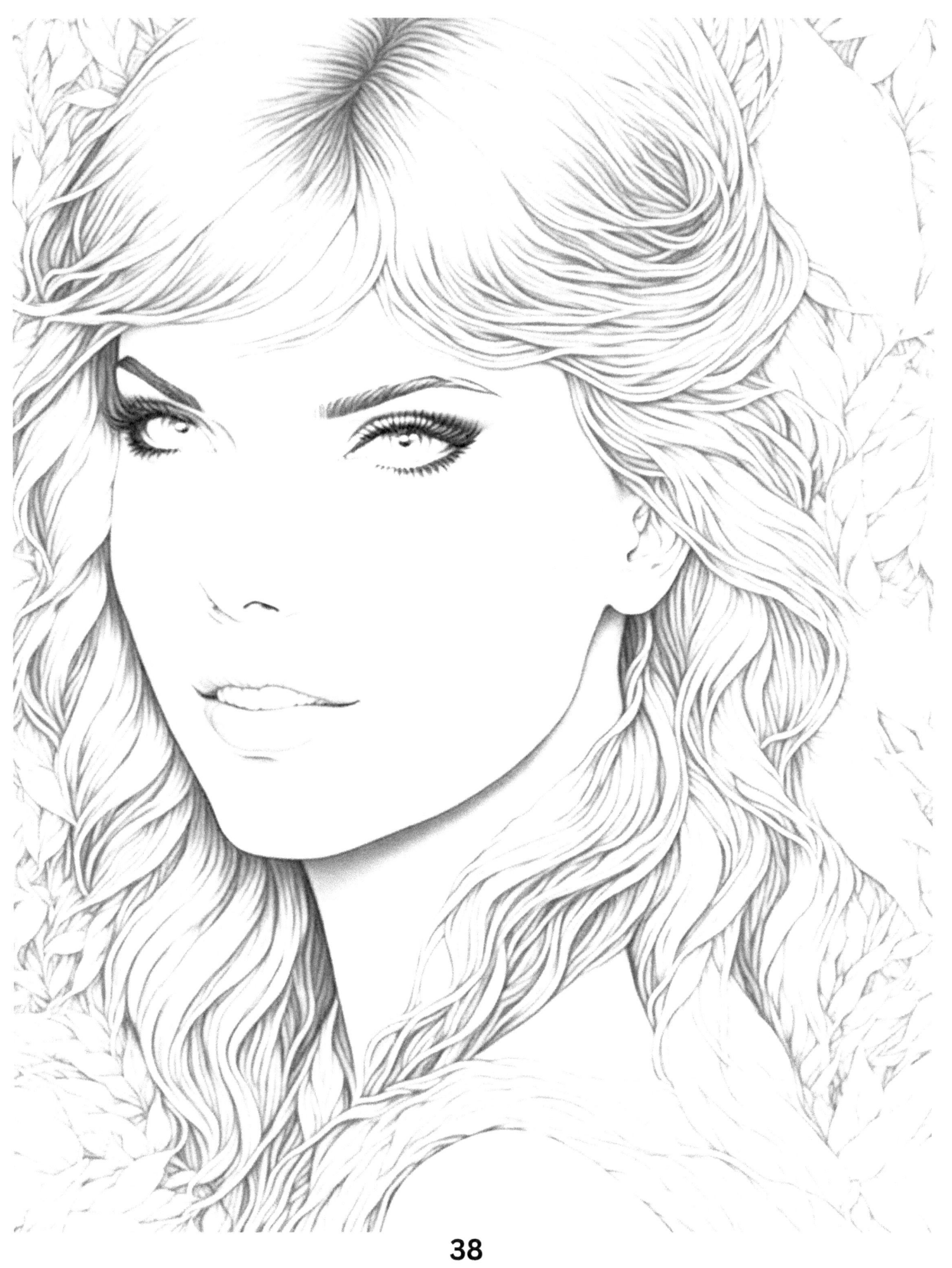

38

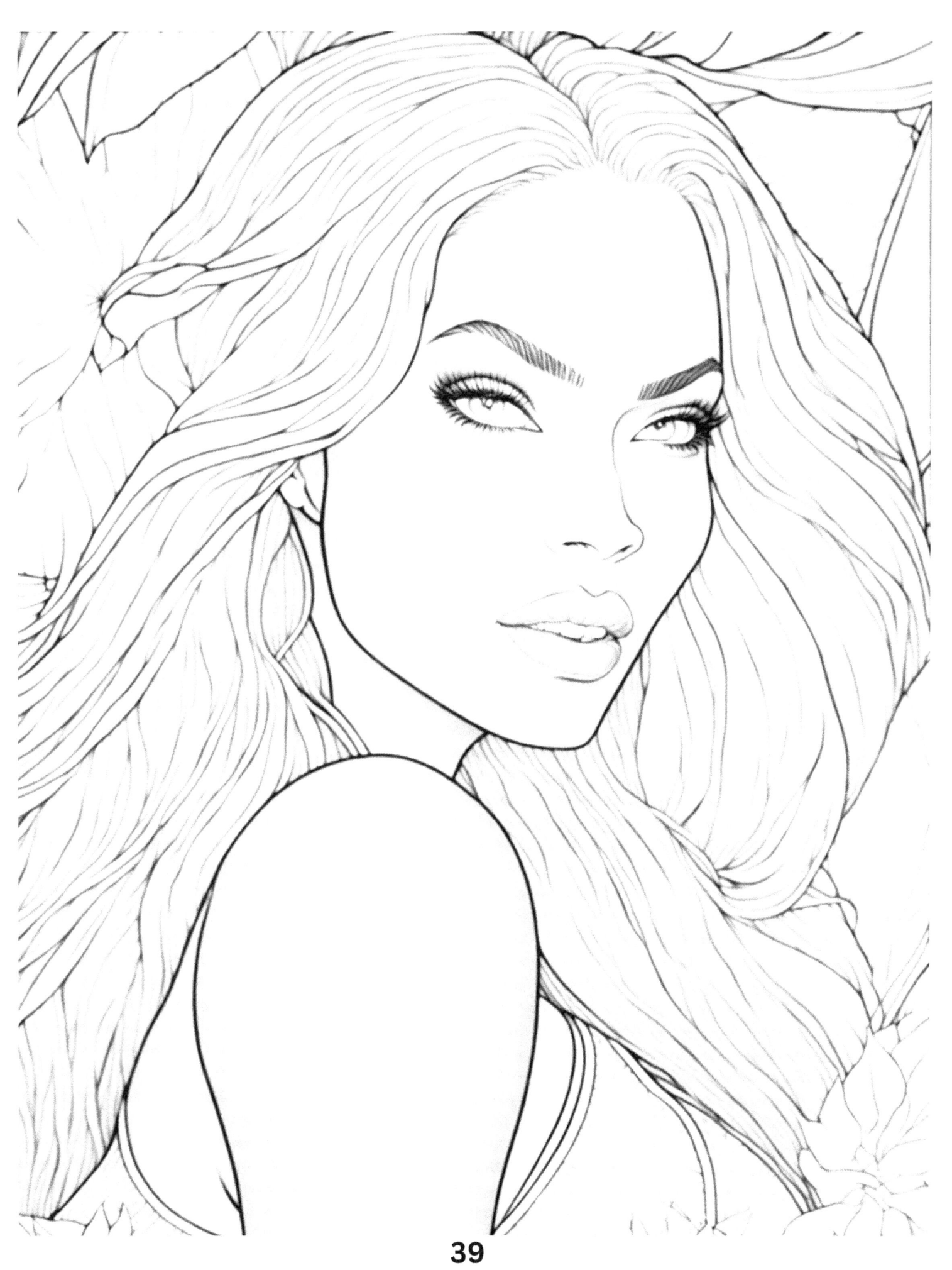

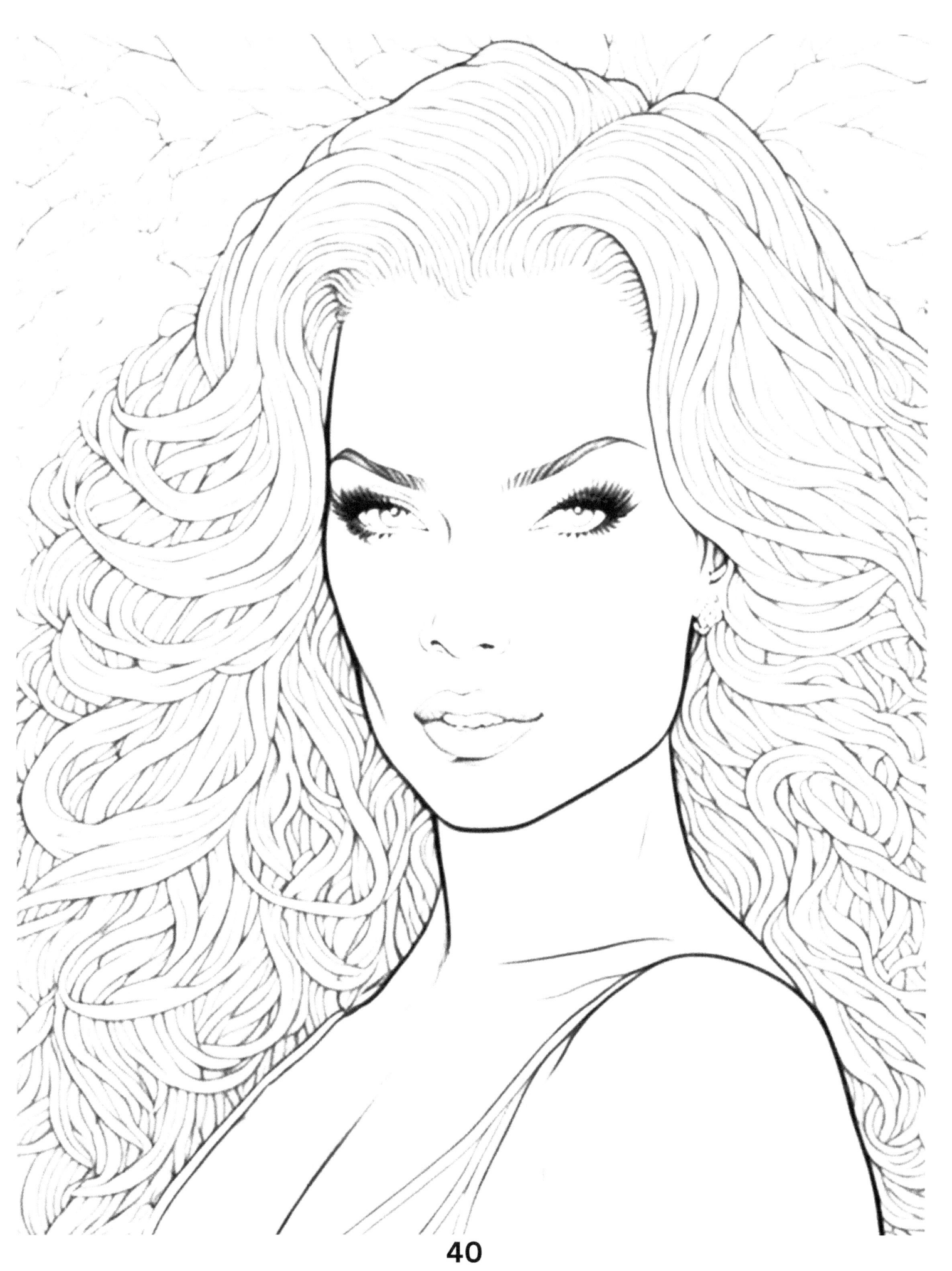

40